MY GAME
MY PAIN | MY PURPOSE

MY STORY OF ABUSE, ABANDONMENT,
ALCOHOL, DRUGS, SEX, AND REDEMPTION

---

*I ran hard and fast to forget my past
and ran right into my purpose.*

KEVIN KIRCHEN

TABLE OF CONTENTS

THE DEAL

I was 17 years old, and my foster parents had just asked me to leave their house. I had no place to go and was couch surfing again. After a while, I decided I would try to stay at my mom's house again. My mom allowed me to come back, but only for a little while, until I found somewhere else to go. Being back at my mom's house just brought up all the old hurts my mom had caused. Now, I had even more hurt, because I had been asked to leave my foster parent's house. I had been living with my foster parents for almost three years. During that time with them, I had been going to church two to three times a week and was part of the church teen group. I had been reading the Bible, praying daily, and had accepted Jesus into my life.

I was just starting to somewhat like my life at this point and had started to accept everything and everyone around me. I just wanted to be loved and accepted. I wanted to live a normal life with a normal family. I wanted to get married at an early age and was even thinking about becoming a pastor.

When my foster family asked me to leave, I was crushed. All my dreams were shattered. I immediately became mad at my foster parents, mad at God, mad at the church, and mad at the world. After I left my foster parent's house, I remember being out, running around, and seeing them. Every time I saw them, it made my stomach churn. I wanted to cry. Eventually, I turned that sadness into a non-caring attitude and eventually started voicing explicit language regarding them to anyone who mentioned their name. Some people didn't understand my attitude towards them. This kind of response was now my protection to hide my sadness. I had even started talking about the church and church people in the same way, because it was one more time someone else had abandoned me. Shortly after, I realized that when I was mean or intimidating, people left me alone. So I decided to keep acting this way. I also decided to try and find someone or something that would never leave me or hurt me anymore.

One weekend, when I was back staying at my mom's house, some of my buddies decided to drive down to San Diego State University for a party. One of my buddies' sister and her boyfriend had invited him and some others down for a birthday party and they asked me to come along. I remember them asking if my mom would let me go and at this point and time, I really didn't care what she thought. We were not talking, so I decided I would just go and deal with her and any repercussions later.

When we finally got to San Diego, the party had already started. Of course, my buddies decided we needed to party fast to catch up with everyone else. I remember everyone there was a few years older than us. As soon as we arrived, we were offered alcohol and drugs. Now, at this point in my life, drug use had been limited to occasional weed smoking, but these people had some drugs I had never used before and I wanted to try them all.

That night was my first time ever doing cocaine or mushrooms. When the cocaine came out, I remember looking at it and thinking I really was somebody now because I was going to do some cocaine. I also was feeling a little nervous because I didn't know what to expect and a little excited because this was a so-called big time drug. Someone rolled up a dollar bill, handed it to me, and said to put one end of the bill in my nose and the other end on the cocaine and snort it up. I did what they said and took the hit. Immediately, I got this burning feeling in my nose and sneezed. It turns out, sneezing was not good, since I blew a nice amount of the cocaine on the floor and now had everyone yelling at me about what I had done. The guy who brought the cocaine didn't yell. He just laughed and put more out.

After that, I did a couple of more lines, then I got the hang of it and I was off and running. I remember drinking a lot of beer and feeling really buzzed from the cocaine. Then a joint came around and I had some of that also. The next thing I knew, out came a baggie with these stems in it. I asked what it was and they said these were mushrooms. I was told it would be a good trip – so, I thought *why not* and then proceeded to chew on some stems. By now, I was so high I went into a bedroom to lay down. When I got to the bed, I saw that an older girl followed me in. She started kissing me and we started to mess around. Then I started feeling extremely high and hot. I didn't know what was happening, so I got up and sat on the edge of the bed and as soon as I did that, the girl left.

Here I was, in the room by myself, sitting on the edge of the bed, and upset because the girl left. Then I started thinking about my life and how I was all alone. I was so hurt thinking about my life that I started to cry and under my breath, started cussing out everyone I had ever known. I was even cussing at God because I felt He hurt me and left me, too. And that's when the devil paid me a visit.

I was still sitting on the edge of the bed when the wall I was facing started moving and distorting in a swirling motion. The wall melted away and opened up to a big hole, and out of this came the devil. I will never forget the image of his big head and ugly face. It was straight up evil. Behind him was a deep space of darkness with fire and smoke. The whole area was so big it looked like I could have got up and walked right into it.

As I sat on the edge of the bed, the devil's face came out of the wall and looked right at me. As he was looking at me, his neck stretched towards me until we were face to face. At that point I was frozen and in shock of what was happening. He just stared into my eyes with this very hard stare, then tilted his head from side to side and said in this deep voice, "F*** God. F*** the church. F*** your foster family. F*** them all. What do you want?"

I thought about it for a minute and said "I want women, money, and power."

Then he questioned me with, "Are you sure?"

I said "Yes!"

The next thing I knew, he let out this wicked laugh and said, "You want it? You got it." Then his head moved back towards the wall and he disappeared. The wall closed up and everything went back to normal. After this incident, I remember sitting on the edge of the bed and wondered what had just happened. Was it real? Was I dreaming? Or was I just high?

I realized then that I was not high anymore. In fact, I was completely sober. A feeling came over me and I knew that I just made a deal with the devil. I remember saying "Alright devil, show me what you got. Let's see if you can make me happy and get me women, money, and power."

There was a part of me that was excited—excited to see what would happen. And another part of me was fearful—fearful because I was now dealing with the devil and deep down, I knew what I had done went against God. I quickly justified what I had done because of all the bad that had happened to me and I told myself I did a good thing because now, I had the devil on my side. I wanted to see how he treated me and if he would fulfill what I had asked for. I also decided what I did was okay because God had let me down and had not been there for me, so why not switch sides?

When I left the room and went back out to the party, I felt very different. I can't explain what that feeling was, except that I knew something had changed. During my limited days of partying, I had always been afraid of getting too high or just plain overdosing. But now, I had no fear and didn't care. It was like I knew that the devil had to keep me around and keep his promise to me since I left God for him.

I partied and partied hard and didn't stop, until I passed out. I just remember waking up the in the morning in my own throw up, laying outside with my head hanging over the balcony. I had a big time hangover, which I had experienced before, but this time was unlike any other. This day everything looked different, including my hangover, and it very quickly went away. When my buddies and I finally drove home, we talked about the night we had and all the crazy things that went on. We always went through who got with a girl, who got in a fight, and who got totally wasted. Then they started talking about how wasted I got and if I remembered them carrying me outside so I wouldn't throw up in the house. They asked if I remembered anything at all and I said, "I think I made a deal with the devil last night."

They all laughed and sarcastically said, "You made a deal with the devil? What did you do, sell your soul?" And then they just laughed some more.

At this point in my life, I was an average looking teen. My hair was shoulder length, I had a gap between my front teeth, stood just over five feet tall, and weighed around 165lbs. I started to occasionally lift weights with my buddies in their garages and before I knew it started to get some muscles on me. Over the next year, my looks completely changed. My body got bigger, my face thinned out, and my voice got deeper, too. I was starting to attract girls that I never thought I would even talk to or hang out with. Younger, older, curvier, and thinner—they were all talking to me. I was even getting invited to parties that before, I would have never been invited to, because I wasn't part of the *in* crowd. Now, all of a sudden, I was a part of the *in* crowd and I was getting all the hot girls. In fact, guys were asking me to go with them to parties because they knew I could get the girls. Wow, was I amazed at the change.

One day, I was hanging out with my girlfriend at the time in her bedroom and saw a Chippendales calendar hanging on her wall. I asked why she had that hanging up and she rubbed the calendar and said, "These are the hottest guys in the world. Look at them! I would do anything to be with one of these guys."

When I heard her say that, I just knew I had to be one of those guys. Later that evening at home, I summoned the devil and said, "Okay devil. I said women, money, and power, so, make me a Chippendales dancer."

Not too long after that, I had made my way up to Redondo Beach, California. I got a job at a local gym and started what would become a life of *women, money, and power.*

Chippendales—
THE BEGINNING

I was 20 years old and now living in Redondo Beach. It had been almost three years since I made the deal and asked for women, money, and power, but by this time, I had completely forgot that even happened. I had just been hired to work at a local gym in membership sales and it was great job. Not only did I get free workouts, I was also dating the aerobics instructor. I remember the day I met another one of the sales man who I would eventually become good friends with. We started training and partying together. Throughout the week, we would go out to these local bars that held hot body contests for men because the bars were always full of girls. The men who entered the contests had to take their shirts off to music while three female judges watched and decided the winner. Week after week, we went to these bars and watched the contests. I would watch because the girls really went crazy for these guys, so I studied what the winners did to win and observed the girls to see who they liked. I also found out that these girls always hooked up with one of the guys after the contest and I wanted to be one of those guys.

One night my friend introduced me to a female friend of his. She was forty, very attractive, and drove a very nice Porsche. I had acquired a phony ID to get me into these bars, so she never really knew how old I was. Over the next few weeks, she and I became very close. She introduced me to black beauties or speed, taught me how to dance seductively, showed me what to wear to the bars, and soon after, we started dating. This went on for a while. The three of us would meet up at the bars and watch the contests together. And each week, I was getting in better shape and my confidence in winning a contest was growing. This was who I wanted to be. I wanted to be someone who girls always recognized and screamed for and these guys had that.

Eventually, during the contests, girls started to ask my friend and I if we were participating. And one night, my new girlfriend asked me to sign-up. My buddy said if I did it, he'd do it with me and I was just buzzed enough to say okay. We put our names down immediately because they only allowed ten guys to compete. I had no idea I was signing up for something that would soon shape my life. I became really nervous looking at these other guys because they were all older than me and had so much experience. This is what they did—they went from bar to bar to compete in these contests. There were already six guys signed up that night. I had seen them contend before and they were all good, to say the least. The bar had a back area where the DJ wanted us to go and wait for them to begin announcing our names. When my buddy and I headed over, all the guys were oiling up, doing pushups, doing dips on chairs, and were even doing pull ups in the men's bathroom stalls. These guys were serious about winning.

The shot girl came by with drinks, so we all had a few and then it was time for the contest to start. The DJ had us pick numbers. I picked number two and my friend was number four. Then two guys I had never seen before showed up. They were both dancers from the club, Chippendales, and of course they drew numbers nine and ten. One was average built and the other was all muscle. Both were good looking and at this point, I knew I was done and I wasn't even going to place. For a minute, I thought I had my competition, knew how they danced, and was hoping for third place, but when these two new guys showed up, I wanted to back out.

After drinking a couple of more shots they asked us to pick the song we wanted to dance to. Everybody had a go to song but me, so I told the DJ to play whatever he wanted to. We all went out on to the dance floor and the girls roared. Man, what a feeling! I really liked it, and this is what I wanted. The bar was packed with girls. Everywhere I looked were girls, and they surrounded the dance floor.

The ten guys entered the dance floor in a line and in order from one to ten. As each guy came out, the girls roared. Some guys got a louder roar than others. When it was my turn to dance and take it off, I didn't know exactly what to do and didn't like the song the DJ picked. But then I remembered what I had seen done before by guys who had won, so I went to each judge and did a little dance in front of them. I took off my shirt nice and slowly, and then I remember something changing inside of me. I was oiled up, pumped up, and feeling numb when in that moment, I heard a voice say, "Here comes the women, money, and power."

When my shirt came off, the girls roared very loudly and when I went back in line, the guys were telling me *nice job* while shaking my hand. Then as each guy went after me, I listened to their applause to determine if I was in the hunt. That's how the winner was decided—by whoever got the loudest response. I felt good about my chances until number nine and ten came out. Number nine was really good, but didn't get much of a response from the crowd. Then came number ten and it was loud as soon as he walked out. He could dance, he was built, and was good looking. When he took off his jacket—bam—it was all over. The girls made so much noise I knew he had won. When the contest ended, they called out each guy one at a time for the girls to make noise and then they announced the winners. Third place went to number nine. Second place went to me—wow! And of course, first place went to number ten.

After the contest, number ten came up to me and suggested I go and audition for Chippendales. He gave me the office number and told me to let them know he referred me. I was in complete shock because this was one of the main men at Chippendales and he was suggesting I go audition. I remember telling the devil to get me into Chippendales and three years later it was happening. I told my friend about the Chippendales audition and he was all for it. If you were a Chippendale, you were it. All women loved the Chippendales men—they were world famous, filled calendars, novelties, cards, TV shows and special appearances—everywhere they went, women swarmed. There were a lot of guys who tried to become Chippendales, but only a few made it. You had to be six feet tall and every night your applause had to be above a seven on the applause meter. Yes, they had an applause meter at Chippendales and it registered noise up to ten. Every night the guys came out on stage and did what was called a *lineup* and if any of the guys received scores below a seven for over a week or two straight, he was usually fired.

The next day I called and spoke with the woman in charge of hiring. I let her know that I was referred by number ten. When she heard this, she invited me in to audition. She said to wear something that showed my body and to bring ID. Everything happened so quickly and the next thing I knew, I was driving up to Chippendales in Culver City for my audition. I was nervous on the drive. Not only did I not want to get turned down, but I still had a phony ID because I had a good six months before I officially turned 21.

The main office was a little shack across the street from the club itself. The woman met me right as I walked in. She was sitting at her desk surrounded by pictures of all the Chippendales. She talked with me for a minute and then asked me to take off my shirt. I remember her saying, "Well, you are handsome and you have a nice body, but you look really young." She then told me I needed a theme or something to go with my young look—something that would make the women go wild. She told me she would give me a shot—one week in the club—to see how the girls would respond to me. I would be announced as the local high school quarterback that was moonlighting after school. Then she handed me the Chippendales outfit—cuffs, collar, black spandex pants—and told me I would start that night.

I remember walking out of the interview on cloud nine. Here I was, 20 years old, and now working at the most famous night club for women in the world. I decided to stay in town since I was starting that night and the traffic was horrible going back to my house. I found a tanning salon and a gym close by. During my workout I kept telling myself I was going to get big, and I was going to be the best. I was going to make it as a Chippendale and at the same time, another part of me was in total fear. Fear that I wouldn't make it, that the women wouldn't like me and that I would be laughed at and rejected one more time. Talk about a crazy up and down emotional rollercoaster. I wanted this so bad because I knew this would make me and I would finally be wanted and noticed. I would finally be admired and my mom would be proud of me. I would be somebody famous and everyone would know who I was. With all that on the line, I could not fail—I had to make it.

After I trained, tanned, and showered, I headed over to the club. It was a Thursday night and I had no idea what to expect, which made me very tense. I remember driving very fast so I wouldn't be late and then when I got close, I slowed way down so I wasn't early. I was a complete wreck with emotions flying all over the place. When I pulled up to the club, women were already lined up waiting to get in. They all looked my way and pointed at my car. The valet met me, and I told them this was my first night. They welcomed me and showed me where to park. As I got out of my car, the women in line started screaming and taking pictures. *Wow.* What a rush. My whole body just exploded with adrenaline. I had excitement, embarrassment, anxiety, and fear all at once. When I entered the club, all I saw on the walls were huge pictures of the Chippendale guys. As I looked around the club I was in awe. I remember thinking, *Man, I've actually been hired and I am one of them.* I had wanted to be a Chippendale ever since I had seen one of their calendars in the bedroom of the girl I dated in high school. You need to understand something, this very club was one of the most famous clubs in the world. The Chippendale dancers stood alone. No one could touch them. They were known as the best-looking guys in the world. All women knew who the Chippendales were and many women had seen them perform, owned their calendar, G-string, or playing cards. If you were a Chippendale's dancer you were an idol. I can tell you this— during that time—even then men were envious of the Chippendales.

They weren't dumb. They knew that if they hung with us they would get the women, too, just by association. The men would be lined up outside the club at least an hour before our last show ended, so they could get inside to mingle and pick up on the women. It was the perfect storm for these guys. There were women inside who had been partying for hours—combine that with watching men strip— and really, it was game over and all the men knew it.

Now it was time to get ready for the first show. As I entered the dressing room I saw the rest of the guys. Whether these guys are hosts or waiters, they totaled around ten. Every guy was either oiling up, doing push-ups, doing pull-ups, or spraying hairspray. I was very intimidated by this because for one, it was my first night. Second, all these guys were a lot older than me, some over 30. But I jumped right in, put on some oil, and did my push-ups. The next thing I knew, the bartender came back with shots and everyone grabbed one. They saluted and welcomed me in. Once I saw that they drank, and it was cool, I immediately ordered a Long Island ice tea to get a little more buzzed before I left the dressing room. I needed to be loose, and I had to be able to talk to these women. I had to make sure they liked me and would applaud for me, and I had one shot to be above a seven on the applause meter.

As I talked to the other guys, I found out that the actual dancers were a separate group of five men. They showed up later, about 30 min before show time. So, the *Men of Chippendales,* as they were called, included five dancers in the L.A. club and five in the New York club. The other 15 guys, in either club, were hosts and waiters. In total, there were only ten Chippendales dancers and around 30 hosts and waiters worldwide.

When I finally left the dressing room, the women were already being seated and ordering drinks. It was my job to walk around and talk to them. I made it a point to sit at all the tables and talk to all the women. They were all wild—some were married, some were getting married, some were already drunk or high, some were wearing very skimpy out-fits—all of them ready to have fun. I remember almost every woman asked me how old I was because I looked very young. A lot of the women made comments about taking me home and breaking me in. I remember being very shy and nervous talking to all these women. I didn't know what to say or how to approach them. All I wanted was for them to like me. I was so nervous about getting good applause in the lineup that I asked every woman to cheer for me because it was my first night. After I had made it known it was my first night, all the woman started calling me *the virgin*.

It seemed like forever waiting for the lineup. The club opened at 6:30 p.m. and the lineup opened the show, which didn't start until 8:30 p.m. I had already been rubbed on, kissed, grabbed, pinched, offered cocaine, offered sex, offered limo rides, and some women even asked me to go home with them. I watched some of the women leave with the waiters and hosts. These women would have sex with the guys either in the men's bathroom or upstairs above the dressing room. I was invited to join in on a few encounters, but said no. I was very nervous and shy— not to mention it was also my very first night, and I didn't want to get caught or fired.

A little later, the main host came up to me and let me know to get ready for the lineup. He told me what number I was and then the music started. The song was "Ladies Night" and the women went wild. The club was so loud and I watched as the women went crazy. These ladies had been drinking and partying for a good two hours or more already, so they were primed for the main event. As each guy came out, they screamed. Some guys got louder applause than others. At this point, I was standing by the woman who hired me, so I could watch the applause meter on the other guys. Next thing I know she asked if I was ready and boom—it was my turn.

As I approached the stage entrance, the MC introduced me as the 17-year-old high school quarterback who was moonlighting. When I heard this, the adrenaline started pumping, and then I hit the stage. The girls went nuts. Wow, what a rush. It was so loud even the other guys looked at me in amazement. Now remember, I did look very young, and compared to all the other guys, I really did look like I was still in high school. The women loved this. When the lineup was done, I went over to ask the woman who hired me how I did and what my score was. She had a big smile and said, "You did great." She showed me that my score was 8.5. I still remember this. Well, that was it! I had done it. I passed the first test. I was in the top five and I did it on a *Thursday*, which was one of the slowest nights of the week. Next up was the weekend—the craziest nights of all.

I just knew Friday night was going to be completely different for me because for one, we had two shows. So, for now, I could slow down a bit and relax. I could have some fun since I had conquered the first night.

During the first show on Friday, things went well and I got another good response as the moonlighting high school quarterback. The woman really liked this and I guessed it was a fantasy for some of them. After the show, I noticed some of the dancers were leaving to go eat. I hadn't had a chance to talk to any of them and that was what I wanted to do—to talk to them and learn how to become a dancer. They were in a different class than the waiters and hosts, they were the dancers these were the guys I wanted to be a part of.

During the break between shows, the waiters got their section together and the hosts just stood around. I had a drink with a couple of regulars who stayed for the second show and I found out later that these women were there almost every night. They introduced themselves and gave me a little more info on the second show. They told me the owner and his girlfriend would be attending. They let me know the second show was always longer, and the women were always a lot crazier since the drugs would be flowing once the club opened to the public.

By this time, the dancers were coming back and I talked to a few of them as they were headed to the dressing room. They welcomed me and asked me to get the girls primed and ready for them. Across the way, by the entrance, I saw the waiters looking outside, so I went to check it out. The women were lining up to get in, and the line went way down the street. As I looked outside at the crowd of women, I noticed these women were a lot younger than Thursday's group. They were dressed skimpier and were completely ready to let it all hang out. They came in packs, they came in limos, they came drunk, they came high, they came ready for anything. It was a madhouse and we were sold out that night for both shows—standing room only.

As they started letting the women in, some went running to get the seats right on the stage floor. The stage floor was in a half circle with bench type seating and there was a rail above it that had more seating. Those were your best seats. Behind that was an aisle way, followed by stadium type seating, with tables and chairs. Then you had the open bar area which was standing room only, too. By the time all the women were inside, some of the women couldn't even see the stage because it was so packed.

Now it was time for me to do my thing. I tried to sit or stand with every group I could and when I sat with a new group, I always ended up sitting on a woman's lap. I was getting grabbed and groped the whole time and sometimes I didn't even know who did it. Eventually I started to notice that the women who came in all respectable and proper were no longer respectable and proper. They were drunk, loud, and some even got sick. Some were passed out and almost all were obnoxious. During this pre-show party, the women would ask to take pictures with me, having me sign their calendars or their body parts and they were not shy about exposing any area they wanted signed. This night was like no other for me. I had never been around anything like this before. Oh, sure I had done that hot body contest in the bar with wild women, but this was completely different. This was it—my new playground.

I worked my way through the crowd of women which numbered way over 250 and was approached by the woman who hired me. She asked me to come with her because she wanted to introduce me to the owner. I had no time to prepare or anything, she just walked me right up to him. He looked me up and down and then told her, "He looks like a baby. Do the women like that?" Just then, a woman came over and grabbed me to take a picture with her and then told me how fine I was. I couldn't have asked for better timing since I was standing next to the owner and the woman who hired me.

Now it was show time. The lights went out and the music started. I remember the roar the women let out as the show started and it gave me goose bumps—it was so loud. The MC came out and did his thing, and after that we started the lineup. I believe I was like number four or five going out and once again he announced me as the high school quarterback who was moonlighting. He added that I didn't have a car and may need a ride home, and that created a huge roar. I came out and the women screamed so loud and for so long that some of the other guys in the lineup bowed to me. I couldn't believe what I was hearing and seeing. This was it for me and with that entrance, I knew I had a good shot at getting hired.

When I came off stage, I went up to the woman who hired me to look at the applause meter and guess what—10. I got a 10 and she said, "Nice job, you did it!" Then the owner came up and shook my hand. That was it. I had made it. I was now officially one of the *Men of Chippendales* after two nights and I never looked at the applause meter again.

Now I was officially in. I worked at the club five nights a week, and one night I was asked to collect the dancers' clothes as they stripped. This meant I sat out on the stage floor in the middle of the women. I didn't like the job at first because I felt I was just being used for grunt work, but then I realized I was able to watch every act this way. I watched each dancer, how they moved, how they took off their clothes, and how they kissed the women when they got tips. I would go through it in my head as they did their act until I had it down. Eventually I was able to do each act in my head. This position also got me in the dressing room to see how the dancers were getting ready. I saw how they put on their costumes and was able to learn every piece of the show.

One night the dancer who did the act known as the *Unknown Flasher* got into an accident and was going to be out for a while. He was the first act and no dancer could replace him since they all had their own personal acts in the show. This was it. This was my in. I told the woman who hired me I knew the act by heart and she was amazed. She had me go through the routine in the dressing room with the lead ensemble dancer. After I did it perfectly, the lead dancer told her to let me do it. By this time all the guys were telling her to give me a shot, and of course she was nervous about the idea, but she agreed and let me do the act anyway. The other dancers helped me get ready, the bartender brought me a couple of drinks, and I was ready to go. Talk about nervous— wow—this moment was more nerve racking than my very first night because tonight, I was stripping.

The costume of the *Unknown Flasher* went like this—I had big over-sized shoes and a long trench coat. Underneath this, I had two pairs of speedos on. The first pair had a question mark on it that lit up and the second pair had two eyes and a tongue that lit up. Beneath this was my G-String. Holding all that up were suspenders, and then to finish it off I had gloves, a hat, and a bag over my head. It was a crazy costume, but the best one for my first-time stripping, because the women could not see my face and I could only see the women through the eye holes of the bag. Nobody could see how nervous I was because I was hidden under the bag. It was perfect.

Once again, the show was starting with the song "Ladies Night", and the women started screaming. Then the lineup came out and the women got crazier. As this was happening, I snuck out of the dressing room and into the crowd to be ready to go on stage. My heart was now pumping out of my chest and the MC said, "Ladies, are you ready for your first dancer?" The ladies screamed, the light lowered and out I went.

As I walked to the entrance of the stage, I heard a voice say, "Here you go, this is what you wanted!" and I knew what that meant. When I hit the stage, it was like Kevin checked out and this other guy took over. The nerves were gone, and I wasn't even thinking about the choreography or stripping. I was completely on auto pilot, like I had done this many times before. As I went through the act, I could see that everyone was watching me, not just the women, but all the other dancers, too. I went through the act flashing and taking items off.

All of a sudden, in the middle of the act, the lights come on and the MC stops me. He tells me I can't be doing all this, and so I scratch my head, shrug my shoulders, and start to take off my shoes. He stops me again and asks about my shoes. I look at my shoes and take one of them off. Then, he grabs the shoe out of my hand and shows it to the women. Now, the shoes I had on were probably a size 20 or larger. The MC says, "If this is his shoe size, can you imagine the size of his…"and the women went crazy. Then he looks at me and says "Well, it looks like they want you to finish, so go ahead." I take the rest of my costume off and I am now down to the bag. To my surprise, Kevin now shows up—no way— what a time for that to happen. My buzz is gone and I am completely aware that the bag has to come off and I have nothing on but a G-String. Well, there was no turning back. I take a deep breath and off comes the bag.

Now comes this thing called *tip and kiss*. This is when the women wave money for a kiss, which means now I have to grab money and give out kisses. I was the first dancer and these women had been waiting for hours for the show to start. They had been drinking and getting all wound up for just this moment and I wasn't prepared for what was about to happen. The women were waving one, five, ten, and twenty dollar bills at me, so I'm grabbing the money and getting mauled at the same time. These women grabbed, pinched, and pulled on every part of my body. They were trying to stick their tongues down my throat, they would put their mouths on my area, they were spilling their drinks on me, and they were completely out of control. Strangely enough, there was a part of me that kind of liked it. Finally, the music stopped, I bowed for the crowd, and the MC came out and said, "The Unknown Flasher—Mr. Kevin Kirchen—and that was it! My first night as a dancer was done. The guy I replaced that night didn't come back for a while and I did the act so well that it was officially mine. I had become the Chippendales dancer I set out to be and it all happened within a few months of being hired there.

I danced in this L.A. Club for another year or so, and during that time I had acquired a need for alcohol each night before I went on stage. I even started doing cocaine. First, I started out with quarter grams, which would last a few nights. And I found out a few things very quickly— that I was at my best when I drank. I tried dancing sober and I didn't feel right—I either felt embarrassed or irritated from being grabbed and mauled, so sober didn't work. Drinking made me uninhibited and I was to be able to handle the obnoxious women because it brought out the other Kevin, the crazy—do anything, didn't care—Kevin. Drinking made it all okay and fun. I felt great and that's what I wanted most of all.

The next thing I found out was that I could not do cocaine before I performed because it made me too jittery and too tight to dance. Eventually, I decided to mix the two together—bad move. For me, this was a nightmare, because I either got too high, because of not enough alcohol, or too buzzed because of not enough cocaine. I never found the perfect combo to dance on, so I put myself on a strict *alcohol only* show diet. Now, the after-show party was a different story because I could let it loose, so, the alcohol cocaine combo was perfect.

During this time span, a couple of things happened that impacted me greatly. To my utter shock, our original choreographer was fired. Shortly after this, a new choreographer was hired out of Las Vegas. These two incidents changed the face of Chippendales and my career forever.

When we all heard about a new choreographer being hired, we also heard he was going to completely change the show. For us, that meant new dancers would be brought in and some of us would stay, while others would go. This new choreographer was going to choose which dancers he wanted to keep and then hold auditions for the host and waiters who he wanted to try out for the show. This guy watched each of our routines for a few weeks, he watched us together, he watched how we interacted with the women, and how they reacted to us. Sometimes, he hung out with us after hours to get to know us better. We always had to be on point because he was given complete control from the owner to change whatever he wanted.

It was a rough, few weeks for me because I wasn't sure if I'd make the cut. None of us were completely sure who he would keep. Then the night came when he posted up the names of the dancers who had made the cut, along with the host and waiters he auditioned. If your name wasn't listed you were out. I looked at the list, hoping my name was on it and— bam, there it was—I was in. It was an emotional night because some of the dancers who had helped me get started and taught me the ropes were not on the list. For them that meant their Chippendales career would end when the new show opened.

The new show was called, *Welcome to Your Fantasy*. It was a storyline of a woman's fantasy night out. There were many different acts in the show and mine was called, *Room Service*, which became the main feature on our promotional video for the eventual U.S. tour we would soon embark on.

Chippendales –
THE TOUR

One afternoon, I was laying on the beach in Venice, California with my roommate at the time and I got a call from the owner of Chippendales asking if I would fly out to Denver right away to perform the *Room Service* act. The owner said "Kevin, I need your help. I need you to come to Denver tonight and do your act." By the time he called me, Chippendales had already been performing in Denver and Phoenix for months and another dancer had been doing this act. I had not been with Chippendales for a few months because the owner got upset and fired me for moonlighting with another dance group, and this in itself is a crazy story. I couldn't believe it would cause me to get fired from Chippendales.

While dancing for Chippendales, I had become friends with a guy who owned another dance group. We had met after one of my regular Wednesday night hot body contests. He was invited to the bar I was doing a contest at by a couple of female regulars who had just met me weeks before. I came to find out later that they had known him for a while and had invited him to see me and set up a showdown contest between us.

We had both heard of each other because both of us had only been beaten once and were both considered to be the best. We talked, had some drinks, did some cocaine, and decided to have the showdown the next week. One of the girls asked which club we would do the contest at – his bar or mine. I quickly told him, "Let's do it at your bar," he laughed and the girls were surprised I had said that because he dominated that bar and had a huge following. I made this decision because I needed an edge and I felt I had a better shot at beating him at his bar than beating him at mine. I knew that since we were both good and known at our home bars that the girls would probably respond well to a new face.

The showdown was set and it was going to happen the following Wednesday at his bar in Woodland Hills. The night of the showdown I was pretty nervous because I didn't want to lose, but I knew how to win, so I just followed my routine like I was in my bar. I found a secluded spot to do my push-ups, pull-ups, and put on my oil so no one would see me before the event began. I needed the element of surprise and for no guys or girls to see me before I hit the stage. The guy I was going up against invited me to do some cocaine, and I knew if I did any before I danced, I would be tight and even more nervous than I already was. So, I turned down the cocaine and decided on a few extra shots to put me into that *lala* state of mind I was used to performing in.

It came time to draw numbers – he drew two and I drew seven. That was a great draw for me because he had to go before me and that meant I could see what he did and how the girls reacted. When they called him out, the women screamed. I watched him do his thing and of course when he was done, the women screamed even more. Then the guys three thru six went and did their thing which did not produce much of a response from the girls at all. While these other guys were dancing, I could see all the girls pointing at me.

Then came my turn and before the DJ could announce my name, the girls started screaming and going nuts, even the girls that set up the showdown. They were chanting, "Kevin – Kevin – Kevin."

I remember the DJ saying, "Alright, Kevin, show them what you got." Then my music by AC/DC started and I did my thing. The girls screamed and went nuts throughout my whole routine and when it was all over, I got first place and he got second. After the contest he asked me if I would do some shows with his group. I agreed and that was it. I danced for his group on the nights I had off at Chippendales and a few weeks after that, the owner of Chippendales caught wind of it and fired me for moonlighting. So, for him to call me up and ask me back was very surprising—one, because the owner wasn't known to bring dancers back and two, because he knew I hadn't done the act in a few months.

During our conversation he said he needed me in Denver that night and that my flight was already booked, so of course I said *yes*. I was very excited to get the call and I knew he would bring me back and keep me on the tour as soon as he heard how I did and how the women reacted. We hung up and I immediately packed some things and headed to the airport. While on the plane, I was trying to remember the *Room Service* act, but couldn't. I was having a lot of trouble remembering the act because it had been a while since I had performed it and I had been doing three or four different acts with the other group.

I landed in Denver and took a cab straight to the club, and by the time I got there the show had already started. I was rushed in through the backway to the dressing room. When I got to the dressing room the dance captain asked me how much of the act I remembered, and I told him I remembered nothing. He immediately popped in a cassette tape with the act's music and called over the ensemble dancers that were in the act to rehearse it with me. By the second time we ran through the act, it had all come back to me and I was ready to go. When I hit the stage, it was like I had never been gone, and that other Kevin kicked in and it was all over. I hammered the act. Afterward came the tip and kiss segment, and the stage was full of women all waving money at me. As I made my way through the crowd, I could see a lady waving a crisp $100.00 bill—man, what a night—and what a way to return. I ended up making great money and had an amazing time back with the old crew.

Later that night, I received a call from the owner of Chippendales who explained that the owner of the Denver club specifically asked if I would be returning. He told me, "You still got it, Kevin, and I need you back and on tour." I had no idea the impact this change would have on my life. That night I returned to Chippendales was the start of a life filled with complete craziness and a fast run toward self-destruction.

The next night I was officially back on the tour and at that time the tour was performing in Phoenix and Denver. Eventually the Phoenix shows ended and we picked up Dallas, but both cities were brutal runs because we only had one night off a week. After one of the shows, the manager told us they had reserved condos for us and that we could live in either Denver or Dallas. He told us all to decide which city we wanted to live in and to let him know within the week. In the meantime, we would be living in the hotels. When we hit each city, I checked out the area, the women, the nightlife, and the access to cocaine. Eventually all the guys chose a city, and most of them chose Denver while only a couple decided on Dallas. As far as our condos went, we were to pay our own rent, utilities, and whatever else we needed. Well when I heard this, I delayed my decision-making process for a good few months, until one of the guys told the manager that I was living in the hotels of each city and that I was the only guy still doing this. I found out that everyone had been watching me and comparing notes which led to them to realize that I didn't reside anywhere. With that I got pressured to make a quick decision—live in Denver or live in Dallas—and after some thought I decided on Denver.

The Denver and Dallas tour was something else. There were so many crazy times and so many crazy stories, but there is one experience that I will never forget. I had only been living in Denver a week or so when some of the guys I lived with invited me to go skydiving. I really didn't want to go but I could not say no so it was on. When we arrived at the jump site they explained to me that I had two choices—choice one was to pay $100 to take a class on skydiving and then jump out of the plane by myself, or choice two which was to pay $250, take no class, and jump tandem with an instructor. I decided on choice two considering I was still hungover from the night before and had just smoked some weed. I also knew I was not going to comprehend anything at all, and I really didn't care to. So tandem it was. The jump instructors had us get dressed while they folded up the parachutes, and as they folded up the shoots, they explained that if the shoots were not folded correctly, they would not open – Really!

As we got in the plane, I quickly realized exactly what I had paid for, which was to jump out of a perfectly good plane at 10,000 feet. When we hit the runway, I knew there was no turning back and the other guys could see I was a bit nervous. The instructor I was jumping with told me to just relax and have fun. He said it was important for me to arch my back when we jumped out of the plane and to stay loose so he could control us.

Once we were at the desired altitude, the plane door opened and the instructor guided me toward the ledge of the door. He had me sit down at the ledge while he got behind me. Then he hooked his harness and attached it to my harness and told me to scoot out of the plane. I was dangling completely out of the plane while he sat on the ledge and the only thing that was keeping us connected were the hooks.

"You ready?" I give a thumbs up and out we went. Here I was, trying to remember everything he told me while in the plane – arch back, stay loose, relax, and so on. Next thing I know, we start spinning, then we start spinning faster, and now the ground begins to look like toilet water swirling. The instructor yells in my ear "I can't get us out of the spin, I can't get us out of the spin! We need to pull the shoot." So, he pulls the shoot and then he screams, "The shoot isn't opening, the shoot isn't opening!" As I look up to see what was happening, I see the shoot just spinning completely flat and doing nothing. I am now thinking I just paid $250 to die and wondering what it will feel like hitting the ground. Then the instructor screams, "We need to pull the other shoot!" I am now thinking *okay*! He really didn't need to tell me that. How about just pulling the shoot? "The shoot isn't opening, the shoot isn't opening!" And now I begin to panic because I see the ground getting closer and the people on the ground are getting bigger, and all I can remember saying was "Come on, God, open the shoot!" The next thing I feel is a big jerk and the instructor laughs and says, "The shoot opened, *hahaha* the shoot opened."

I would like to say everything was much better after the shoot opened, but it wasn't. We were so low in altitude that we hit the ground very fast and hard. This knocked the wind out of me, and we rolled and rolled, twisting all over each other. When we finally came to a stop, we both just sat there on the ground stunned. I was trying to get my breath back and all he wanted to know was if anyone filmed it. As we sat on the ground, some others who had seen what had happened came running to help us. When we got back to the bunker I had so many people ask how I was—they were all scared because they witnessed us spinning and the shoots not opening. Then one lady came up to me and said it was nothing but a miracle that I was ok, and that I definitely had someone protecting and watching over me. When I took her statement in, I realized that I had called on God to help me in that moment and not the devil. Now as crazy as it sounds, this experience didn't stop me from jumping. I jumped again the next week, and two more times after that. Why? Just because.

After a few months, the owner decided to stop the Denver and Dallas shows and take the tour across the entire U.S. and Canada. Almost immediately, we were sold out weeks and even months in advance. I found out later that the owner and management had been working on this tour for a while because the Denver and Dallas shows were not selling out anymore. And just like that the new tour was born. We went hard and fast. I was in a different city every night and a different state every couple of nights. We traveled constantly and eventually I was on the road 40-45 weeks a year. By the time I left the U.S. tour I had performed in almost every state, every major city, and almost every suburb in the U.S. and Canada. We were like rock stars—we sold out everywhere we went, we did radio shows, talk shows, newspaper interviews, and even the local news programs, all to promote the tour. We took the world by storm and everyone knew who we were. It was a time that will never be duplicated or reproduced. It can't be since we were the originals bad boys from the west coast to the east coast and everywhere in between.

Looking back on it now is like a blur—one day blended into the next. I remember at times not knowing what city I was in—that's how fast the road life was for me. Every time we traveled to a new location I either partied, slept, or passed out, while we traveled by bus and or airplane to every destination. The tour bus we traveled in slept 12 and we each had our own bunks. I always had the middle bunk because I could just fall into it and roll out of it easily. The bus was a tour bus for some and a party bus for others. The front of the bus was for the social partiers and the back of the bus was for the steroid shooting, alcohol drinking, weed smoking, cocaine snorting, pill popping partiers. Of course, we did have the few guys that didn't party at all and would judge those who did, but for the most part, we all partied in some way and some more than others, but not too many like me.

I recall times when I would go directly to my bunk, turn on my light, close the curtains, put on my headphones, and snort my cocaine by myself. I had times in my bunk when I got so high I wouldn't leave my bunk until we arrived at the next destination. It was like partying in a coffin, but I wanted the other guys to think I was asleep so no one would know I was still partying or would ask me for any of my stash. Many times, I even shot my steroids in my bunk. How crazy is that, being in a bus doing cocaine and shooting steroids? For me, the bus sometimes became my enemy because I would get so loaded and have no place to go. The night bus runs were like a double-edged sword. I had to party because that's what I did, but I really didn't like to party because everyone was around and watching everything going on. Plus, I really didn't like to sleep on the bus because I didn't trust the driver would stay awake. Every bus trip we made always involved partying, music, gambling, and war stories for at least the first few hours.

Many times, there would be contests between some of us to see how many women we could have sexual encounters with before we left the venue. In one town, I had multiple women within one hour. I am not saying this to brag or boast. I just want you to get an idea of how crazy we were, how crazy life on the road was, and how unbelievably crazy the women were. These women knew we were leaving town in an hour, and would see us going to rooms with other women and would still wait to be with us. I had women actually ask me if I had just had sex with another woman, who just left my room as they were coming in, and when I said *yes,* they still came in. I had women say they knew I had just had sex with a certain woman but didn't care because they would be better.

I had women doing sexual things in the parking lots, restrooms, elevators, kitchens, supply closets, and even in wide open hallways, as I was headed to the lobby to check out. We had women get on the bus and be with multiple guys before we left, and we had women who would do anything and I mean anything to have sex with us before we left town. A few times we even got the bus drivers and stage crew involved in the action. These women were either married, getting married, had boyfriends, or were single. If they were on the prowl, it didn't matter who they were having sex with that night, as long as they were somehow with one of the men who were a part of the show. At the time all of this seemed very wild, very cool, and no big deal to me. As you read this, you may think the same, but as I look back at these times, they actually had a very big impact on me and started to shape and even re-enforce my negative outlook on women, trust, and relationships.

Every time we arrived at our new destination the guys would either eat, take a nap, shop, find a gym, and or find a place to tan. A couple of hours before the show, we would all meet up at the venue for a quick rehearsal before heading back to our room to get ready. We all were paired up and shared rooms, except for the road manager since he usually had his own room. I usually had an extra room for the *after-party Kevin.* Even though we had rooms provided by Chippendales, I rarely stayed in them because of my roommate. I knew I would be up partying and having sex all night and he wouldn't be able to sleep. Some nights wound up to be really insane and when this happened I went to a completely different hotel or if possible, the woman's place.

The show itself was phenomenal. It was a Broadway type show and each guy was perfectly matched for each act. We didn't have all buff guys or all tanned guys or even all fit guys. We had a mixture of guys who worked to attract every woman's desire. Every guy was good looking in his own unique way and every night was different, so you could go from the most wanted to the least noticed in one night. We had the opening act and finale which we all participated in and in-between, there were about eight different acts which included some solo acts.

The solo acts were the tip and kiss acts and you never knew what to expect. You could go from making enough money to feed a small village one night, to needing to borrow some money for the bar the next. I could usually tell how the night was going to go by the applause we got in the opening act. This didn't necessarily mean we would make a lot of money in tips, but it did mean the after party would be mind blowing. Some nights the women were insane and so was the money, but then there were nights when the women were just as crazy, but they did not tip very well. There were other nights where the women seemed dead and gave no applause, but threw money like it was coming off a money tree. It truly was a crap shoot when it came right down to figuring out the crowds, but I can say this, when they were crazy, they were crazy.

I had become pretty good at knowing about how much I had made in tips even before my act was over because I knew I could fit 100 one dollar bills in each hand. Once my hand was full, I had a bucket to put the rest in. It wasn't unusual to have a hand full of money filled with $5, $10, $20, $50, or even $100 dollar bills. You always looked out for the big bills and gave extra attention to the girls who dished out $10 bills and higher. There was a lot of money flying around during those shows and I had become so addicted to substances and alcohol that my money was sometimes gone by the end of the night. I lived on the fact that I could make more the next night, so—what the hell—Let's party, there's always tomorrow and it is only money, right?!

This was my life for the four years I toured the U.S. and Canada and towards the end of that time I started to lose control of my partying and even missed some shows due to being too high. I remember a couple of times being in my room in- between shows and had my cocaine delivered to me. I over shot the mark or snorted too much too quick and just got stuck. I couldn't move or think, so I drank to come down before the show and that didn't help much because now I was just plain trashed. I would call the manager and say I was sick or that I ate something bad, and I would tell him he would need to cut my act that night. I will never forget the night I was in Louisiana to do a show and the night prior I had called a girl I knew to tell her I was coming into town and to bring some cocaine. When I arrived at the hotel in Louisiana she was already there waiting in the lobby for me and had the cocaine on her.

She had gotten a suite for us and was ready to party all night long. I was still a bit wrecked from the night before and decided that some drinks and just a little cocaine would make me good. That brilliant idea didn't work out well for either of us because she came big—she had a good half ounce of jet fuel and one of my notorious half gram lines put me on the ceiling. Naturally, some drinks and some sex were next up, and by the time that was over I was spent. I remember looking at the clock and it was almost show time—not good. I knew I was way too high, and way too buzzed to do the show, but was still going to try. The next thing I knew, I had this terrible stomach ache that had me in the fetal position, so I had this girl call the manager for me and tell him I was really sick. Of course, she wasn't too happy considering she had drove a long way to see me, the show, and have a good time, but now she was just sitting in a hotel room with me while I was being sick. I remember the cramping got really bad and I didn't know what to do, but I didn't care. I just partied right through the pain until all the cocaine and alcohol was gone.

When morning came, I was still in tremendous pain, and was still so high and drunk I decided not to ride the bus to the next town and by doing that I had to get really drastic with my story. I told the manager I was flying back to L.A. to see a doctor.

When I got to L.A., I went to the emergency room to get checked out. They did some tests on my stomach and said they needed to do even more testing and that I would need to admit myself into the hospital. After a couple days in the hospital and a lot more tests, I was diagnosed with Crohn's disease. They told me that I had almost five feet of bad intestines and that they were going to put me on steroids. When I heard steroids, I got pretty excited until I was told they were not anabolic steroids and that these steroids would cause me to retain water and get puffy. That's not what I was expecting, since this all started as a game to make sure I could cover my butt for missing a show when I was high. Now, I was being diagnosed with Crohn's disease.

After the hospital stay and a couple of weeks off work, I joined back up with the tour and I was not the same. I felt sluggish from the medication and my face was so puffy I looked like I had a quart of milk in each cheek. I was not very happy about my swollen face and I really hated how tired I had become. To top it all off, the doctor said I wasn't supposed to drink alcohol while on the medication, so my night life was shot. After about a week, I decided to stop taking the medication and get back on my anabolic steroids and some water pills to get me back in my groove. I rolled the dice with my heath and really didn't care what would happen to me by getting off the meds. I just wanted to get back in shape and party.

Soon after my return, I was called by the owner to dance in the New York club. He needed me to replace one of the guys who had gone on the first leg of a new tour that was opening in Australia. I danced in the New York club for about six months before being called again, and this time, I was asked if I wanted to go to Africa. How cool was that. Of course, I said *yes*. They assembled the group in L.A. and we rehearsed for about two weeks before flying out. We flew from L.A. to London and from London to Johannesburg which was about 21 hours. Then we hitched a ride to Cape Town which was where we were going to perform for six months. We were already sold out for the entire six-month show—two shows a night, Monday through Friday, and three shows on Saturdays for six months. When we arrived at the hotel we were not even checked in before another guy and myself decided to go on a hunt for some weed. This was a bit crazy since we had only been in Africa for a short time and did not speak the language, but within minutes we found our man.

He motioned us to a van and we got in and rolled out. At this point I was a bit nervous because for one, I had no idea where we were headed or how to get back to the hotel, nor did I even recall the name of the hotel. For two, neither of us spoke their language and we were Americans carrying a lot of cash. The van drove down this dirt road for a while before it finally stopped, and now we were in the middle of nowhere. We got out of the van with this guy and he motioned for us to follow him. As we walked I saw mud huts, ox, along with women carrying clothes and food in baskets on their heads. I remember thinking wow—we are in Africa and I have no idea how to get back to my hotel. What if we die out here? No one would find us. Next thing I know, this guy makes a gesture for money, and I didn't want to spend a lot and get ripped off, so I gave him $20. He had us wait for him at a bus stop, which was on the dirt road and beside a little sign, and when he finally came back, he was carrying five large manila envelopes stuffed with weed.

Now what? What was I supposed to do with five huge envelopes of weed, and how was I supposed to get this stuff into the hotel? I had no idea. The next thing I know he's making gesture to smoke some, and I am thinking how can we do that with no papers, no pipe, nothing! But we wanted to smoke so I figured he had a plan. Oh, he had a plan alright! The next thing I know he is pulling out a piece of newspaper, then takes one of the envelopes and pours all the weed onto the newspaper, then he rolls up the newspaper and lights it. I started laughing, but he was serious. We sat at the bus stop and smoked this newspaper size joint, then the other guy and I stuffed the remaining envelopes in our pants and headed back to the hotel.

When we got back to the hotel, we still had to check-in and of course I was a bit nervous considering what we were carrying. Of course, everything turned out fine and we headed to our room. We stayed in bungalows that were attached to a casino which is where our shows took place. So here I am in Africa staying in a casino hotel that never shuts down with I don't know how much weed, and now all I needed to do was find my African coke dealer and it would be game on. Eventually I found my dealer and many other substances along the way.

Africa to me was like any other place, and my routine was the same— music, women, drugs, steroids, and daredevil moves. The experience of living in Africa was something I will never forget. It was a beautiful place and I was able to do and see a lot of amazing things. Things like going on safaris, riding horses on the Indian ocean, feeding baboons, feeding monkeys from my balcony, watching elephants walk the golf course, and so on—I have to say it was a blast. Oh, and did I mention I could have been torn apart by a lion? Yep.

How this came about was, while on a safari, we were asked who wanted to pet the lion cubs and of course I said that I would. Now, these lions were in a different controlled area that was caged in, but they were still lions. As I entered the area, the safari leader told me to not make any sudden moves and to relax because it was the safest time, since the lions had just eaten. As I bent down to pet one of the lion cubs, I felt this brush up against my legs and then two huge paws came over my shoulders. The next thing I feel are a lion's claws right up under my chest muscle. As this lion is pressing his claws into my chest he puts his head right next to mine, shows me his long sharp teeth, and lets out this low growl. After he growls at me, he stays on my shoulders and just stares at me, and by now, I knew better than to make any eye contact with him. At this point that wasn't an issue considering I was completely frozen and in full prayer to God pleading that I don't get killed right then and there.

As this is going on, the safari leader tells me not to worry and just to be calm. He advises me to not move fast, and then I would be ok. And I am thinking—nice, thanks for the speech! Now could you just get the lion off of me?

Here I was in a cage, by myself, with a full-grown lion on my back, his claws in my chest, his teeth inches from my face, and I was being told not to worry and just to be calm? All I could do was pray – God please get this lion off of me right now— and just like that, the lion got off of me and laid with his cubs.

You would think that was it for life threatening experiences, but on that same safari I was almost attacked by a rhino. Towards the end of the tour in Africa, I was almost attacked by baboons, was banned from the casino for fighting, and to top it all off, I was jumped by a van full of guys for my money and passport. As you can see, I could have died many times while in Africa. I even experienced my body shutting down and almost going into convulsions one morning after a huge cocaine party.

When the African tour ended, I joined the European tour, and this tour completed the final years of my career with Chippendales. I traveled all over Europe for almost two years before finally planting in London, where we were booked at the Strand Theatre for months. By the time it was all over for me at Chippendales, I had seen more, done more, traveled more, and made more than most people do in a life time. I partied with the best of them, rock stars, actors, dancers, athletes, and the list goes on. One night, while in Switzerland, I drank whiskey and partied with Johnny Cash, Waylon Jennings, and Willie Nelson. I would say that one topped them all.

There were so many additional stories that took place during my touring years at Chippendales, and as I write this book, I can't even come close to telling you about them all. There were some good ones, some bad ones, some unbelievable ones, and some that I can't even repeat. I will say that the people, places, and parties all became one big haze. It was a part of my life that went by so fast that by the time I finally quit I felt like a racehorse that was rode too hard and put away wet. I partied and ran like there was no tomorrow, keeping my foot on the throttle, and living for the moment. I didn't care about life or death. All I cared about was the next dollar, the next woman, and the next high. I was right where the devil wanted me. I thought I was in control. I thought

I was making everything happen. I thought I was death defying and all the time I forgot the deal I had made. Women, money, and power—that was the deal. The devil was using me to try and destroy others while trying to take me out at the same time, *but* God never let me go. He had another plan for me and my life!

There is no doubt in my mind as I look back on all my experience with Chippendales that God was right there in the midst of every situation covering me, protecting me, and keeping me for a time as this. It was only and is only by the grace of God that I survived those years and am alive today to write about it. None of this is about me. Oh sure, I was a Chippendales dancer and I toured the world, but I was a lonely, out-of-control kid in a man's body. I was addicted to drugs and alcohol, I was addicted to sex. I was addicted to looking good, I was an adrenaline junkie and eventually, I became someone who, through these experiences, became very hard and really didn't care about anyone or anything. It was all about me, it was about who and what I could get. In the process, I hurt many people, I made many people mad, I destroyed many relationships, and many times, I didn't even realize I was doing it. I burned through everything—women, money, friendships, and relationships—life was just like it was the next city over. I became what I hated as a kid in others—I was a destroyer and abandoned others. I was doing the devil's work in facilitating evil, immorality, betrayal, adultery, lust, perversion, and greed. I became an idol to many and an idol of myself. I did almost everything wrong and rarely had any self- convictions. I ripped through almost every commandment. There were even times when I would try to share what I knew about God to try and help someone else in need while I was getting high with them. I was completely out of my mind. One minute playing with the devil and the next trying to help someone get to God. Through it all, as I look back at the crazy and sometimes insane things I did, I see that nothing I did ever separated me from the love of God.

You see, I knew God was real from an early age and I accepted Jesus at an early age. I read the word of God and prayed at an early age, so He was with me through all my *stuff* later on in life. In fact, He knew what I was going to do before I did it and He still never left me. He was my protector. Even being mad at Him, cussing Him out, and deciding to go the other way, He never stopped loving me and protecting me. That is why I say this book isn't all about me. It's all about God and how He kept me, so sure it's my story, but it's about God's glory. All of this is a testimony of God and His unconditional love for me, no matter how far down the road of destruction I went. He knew in the end it would all be for His glory. He knew that what the devil meant for my destruction would end up as a story of redemption.

"Tall, Dark, and
HANDSOME"

Shooting the "Tall, Dark, and Handsome" video was another crazy time during my career at Chippendales, even though the shoot was only three days long. This was one more drama-filled time which had me on another emotional roller coaster ride. I had already been at Chippendales for a while now and had no reason to feel as uneasy as I did, but I did. This was a bigtime moment for me and Chippendales, and during the days leading up to the shoot I was constantly reminded of this by the owner, the choreographer, and even some of the other dancers.

The owner came up with the idea of making a promo tape for the new show, and he wanted to send it to club owners, news stations, radio stations, and every other media outlet across the country. His plan was to create a demand for us to perform in other cities and boost ticket sales. The choreographer and the owner decided that the act they would use for the promo piece would be my act called, *Room Service*. I had been performing the act in Denver and in Phoenix when I got the call that they chose my act for the promo. When I was told my act was the one they would use, I was very excited, very proud, and very nervous. I was to fly to L.A. for three days to film the act, and after the filming I was to fly directly back to Denver for a show that night.

I wasn't happy at all about the slammed schedule and really wasn't happy that I was filming this piece during my days off. Not only was I going to be in L.A. for three days to film the act in a hotel, but I also had to perform the act in the club every night because they needed to film the women screaming, cheering, and getting crazy during the tip and kiss segment.

Before I left for L.A., I was told the owner had hired a female actress to be in the video with me and that her name was Judy Landers. When I heard this, it was all good and the whole missing my days off thing didn't matter anymore. As soon as I landed in L.A. it was on. From the airport I went directly to my hotel, unpacked, called my dealer, picked up my cocaine, and headed to the club to perform.

It wasn't until I arrived at the club that I realized I had to do my act with the L.A. ensemble dancers instead of my tour dancers. Now this situation made me even more uncomfortable, self-conscious, and nervous than I already was. How crazy is that? Here I was, an established lead dancer who had always received great reviews and every time I was put into a pressure situation, I felt inadequate and insecure. Every time I had to perform under pressure, I always felt less than, like I wasn't good looking enough or couldn't dance as well as the other dancers. So, having the pressure of this promo video on me and having to dance with an unfamiliar crew made me very uneasy and the uneasy Kevin only knew one thing to do. Drink!

I needed to get at least a couple of shots of whiskey in me before the quick pre-act rehearsal with the other dancers. I had no time to rest or unwind from the flight, so when I arrived at the club I headed directly to the bar and grabbed a couple of shots and a beer. When I hit the dressing room I had to get into full costume, do the entire act, and strip down to my T-back thong all within minutes of the live filming. Talk about insanity, this was insanity. I had only danced with two of the five dancers who were in the act with me and that was at least six months earlier. We only had a couple of run-throughs to get it right and we had to do it in this small, cramped, and hot dressing room. When we finished the rehearsal, I was a sweaty mess, I barely had time to wipe down and get dressed again before we had to perform it live.

As I was getting dressed, one of the waiters came back with a tray full of shots asking if we wanted any—completely dumb question to ask me! In fact, the waiter even said 'I know I don't have to ask you, Kevin!" We all grabbed a shot or two, saluted each other, and got ready for showtime. When we hit the stage, it was like we had never been apart—we danced, I stripped, the women went nuts, and when it was all over, we had nailed the act. Back in the dressing room, after the performance, everyone was hyped up about how well the act went, including the choreographer, and while I was in the corner counting my money, I caught the eye of the owner and all he did was nod his head and smile.

After the night of filming, Chippendales turned into the usual bar scene and a few of us just hung out and drank. After a bit, I needed to head to another bar by myself to party and find some women. I didn't want to hang out any longer with the dancers or the women from the show because I did not need any *Kevin* stories getting back to the owner or choreographer. So, I headed back to the bar at my hotel and the night went deep into the next morning. Even when I knew I had to be up early to film, this never stopped me from drinking or having cocaine. If I had cocaine and there were women, it was always go time and this night was no different—I wasn't going to stop. Throughout the night, I kept telling myself *this is the last line* and *this is the last drink,* but of course that didn't happen. By this time in my life the cocaine, the alcohol, the women, and partying lifestyle had already taken complete control of me and if I had it, I did it, and I always finished whatever I had no matter what faced me later.

Considering how big this shoot was and how big my part was, it was common sense to not party until the filming was over. I should make sure I was rested, on point, and looking good. I, unfortunately, never entertained common sense when it came to alcohol, drugs, women, or steroids—I was always in full throttle mode. So, the next morning was another *pull it together* Kevin moment—I was sexed up, drugged up, hungover, and so tired, but I could not show it. I had to gather myself and head to the hotel for filming, and luckily for me the choreographer decided to shoot a piece of the ballroom dance scene first which gave me extra time to sleep.

We shot the *Room Service* hotel piece in three days at one of the high-rise hotels in Universal City. The piece involved Judy Landers having a fantasy dream about ordering room service from a young guy. When she wakes up from the dream, she's in the Chippendales club and the young guy she was dreaming about was me, and now I am stripping in front of her.

When we finally finished the three days of filming, I wasn't ready to pack up, jump in a cab, and fly back to Denver to perform again that night—so, I changed my flight. I called the tour manager and told him I was beat and needed some rest. I told him that I would return to the tour a day later than scheduled. I remember he wasn't too happy about that considering he would have to change my act in Denver to a non-tip and kiss act and get a backup ensemble dancer to perform it. After a back and forth conversation with him, he agreed to give me the time. I fully intended to get a good night's rest and relax at the hotel until I had to fly out the next day, but then came the call to go party with some of the L.A. guys that night and one more time it was on. Knowing I had all night and a good portion of the next day to party and sleep, I took advantage of it. I partied so hard that I got zero sleep—in fact, I got on the flight still a bit drunk and still a bit high.

The flight to Denver seemed like one of the quickest flights ever and before I knew it the stewardess was waking me up for landing. When I got off the plane, I hit the airport bar and had a quick drink to get me going. Then I caught a cab and headed directly to the club for the show.

When I arrived at the club, I ordered a couple more drinks to keep me going, and as I was having a drink, one of our tour managers approached me and asked why I wasn't at the show the night before. I told him I was tired from three days of filming and decided to stay in L.A. an extra day to rest and that's when things got a bit heated between him and I. At this point, the conversation had moved into the dressing room and that's when he got in my face and said, "I had a lot of women at the show last night here to see you, Kevin, and you were not here—and if you ever do that to me again you will never dance again!"

I didn't take too kindly to that threatening statement or him being in my face, but I had to stay cool because other dancers were around. So, in a low sarcastic voice I said, "I don't know who you think you are, or who you think you're talking to, but don't threaten me or my job, man! Don't you know that you need me more than I need you? Do you not realize all I need to do is make one phone call and I can get you fired? I can even make a call and be dancing for another group by tomorrow, so get out of my face." This is when he made a statement I will never forget.

He said, "No, Kevin—you don't understand that when I said you will never dance again that's what I meant—you will *never* dance again." He smiled and walked away.

It wasn't until weeks later when our tour flew into Phoenix for a few shows at the Celebrity Theatre that I realized what he actually meant by that statement. This manager, who I had a confrontation with, always picked us up at the Phoenix airport and drove us to the venue or hotel, but on this particular day, he wasn't there. After waiting and waiting at the airport for him to show up, I finally decided to make a call to the theatre to find out where he was.

When I called the theatre where we were performing, a woman answered and told me that this manager wouldn't be picking us up because he had been sentenced to prison for a conspiracy to commit murder. His sentence was for ten years. I remember my heart sank when I heard that because this was the same guy who said I would never dance again. Later that night, I found out from someone close to him that he was going to have my legs broken if I missed another show. I also found out that this man was a part of an even bigger group of players who the owner was involved with and that these guys had some control regarding the Chippendales tour and its dancers.

Not long after this man went to prison, all the dancers including myself started getting handed subpoenas on random nights in different cities as we either came out of the dressing room or offstage. This was because of a lawsuit that was filed by the old choreographer, Nick De Noia, against the owner and Chippendales for the touring rights. Apparently, the owner owed Nick a lot of money and told him he would pay the debt by giving him the tour rights not thinking we would ever tour. So, when we eventually started touring and selling out everywhere, Nick wanted to get paid. Soon the subpoenas stopped being served and a bit after that, we heard Nick had been murdered in New York City.

With all the stuff that happened during the filming of *Room Service*, all the drugs, all the alcohol, missing the one show so I could *relax*, and mixing that with my conflict with the now imprisoned manager for conspiring to commit murder and Nick getting murdered in New York City was completely overwhelming and stressful.

I can only again say— But God!

But after all the dust settled, I really didn't give it much more thought. I just went on as usual with my wild and crazy life—when the truth is, it was all God right there—one more time. He was covering me, showing me mercy, and protecting me from me. How many times would He need to save the crazy, high, drunk, didn't give a damn, Kevin?

The 1993 Chippendales
CALENDAR

The 1993 Chippendales calendar shoot took place in the summer of 1992 in Tahiti. This was the first time I had ever been asked to be a part of a Chippendales calendar shoot so, of course, it was another nerve-racking first for me. Every summer, the owner would ask men to test shoot for the upcoming calendar and every year I anticipated my name coming up and every year I was denied, but 1992 was different. The owner did not ask me to test shoot, but he said, "I want you in the calendar, Kevin." Wow—he really wanted me in it and I knew this was my only shot because he had not asked me before, so if I failed, he would not ask me again. I also knew I had to make the calendar because my time at Chippendales was coming to an end, and not because I was getting old or because I partied too much, but because it was time for me to retire. I was getting burnt out with the traveling, the partying, the women, and the show itself was getting to me. It was no longer fun—it had become annoying and it had become a ball and chain that dragged me around anywhere it wanted.

I had already achieved everything that was achievable with Chippendales by this time in my career, except the calendar. I was in my eighth year at Chippendales and had been on everything from birthday cards, posters, T.V. shows, talk shows, radio shows, and videos. I had been involved with every kind of promotional event possible across the country, so this was the last piece to my career, and I was finally getting my shot.

During this time, the owner had switched from using only Chippendales men for the calendar to using both Chippendales men and freelance models. I knew the owner pretty well and I believe he made this switch to save money, because by using the men of Chippendales he would have to pay and pay well, but using freelance models he would be able to save money. He always pushed the fact that anyone in the calendar would have huge recognition and be known more than any dancer, because it was sold in more countries than we performed in, and at that time, the Chippendales calendar was the world's most famous calendar.

So, my nervousness was legitimate because nothing was guaranteed with him. Oh, of course he asked me to shoot the calendar and said he wanted me in it, but if my pictures were not what he wanted, I knew he would not use them. I had to be on point—body, hair, tan—and I set out to not only make it onto a month, but also a full-page spread and possibly the cover. I told myself I needed to stay sober for the two weeks leading up to the shoot so I could be at my best. Staying sober for those two weeks sounded like a good idea at the time, because by now, I really wanted to stop the cocaine, drinking, and crazy night life. I really thought this would be a good motivator for me and that I would be able to pull it off. I quickly found that my desire for the fast life was stronger than my desire to stop.

I was very anxious during the weeks leading up to the shoot and staying sober for that long wasn't working out well for me. Sober for me equaled being very uncomfortable, so I decided to just keep on partying. I told myself I could quit the drugs and alcohol later and reasoned that my new party session was to celebrate the calendar shoot since I was soon retiring from Chippendales. So, like any other day, week, month, or year, I partied almost every night leading up to the shoot. I partied so much that I didn't even workout leading up to the shoot because of massive hangovers—but, I was always made it a point to at least shoot my steroids and catch a tan somewhere. I was basically on one continuous high—I even went to the airport high, knowing I could sleep it off during the long flight.

When I arrived in Tahiti, I took a cab to the hotel, and while I was checking in, some of the other guys who arrived a few days ahead of me were in the lobby signing up to go scuba diving. After I had checked in, they asked me if I wanted to go with them. Now, scuba diving was something I always wanted to try, but I was really afraid of sharks. I knew if I was ever going to do it, now would be the best time, since I was still wiped out and hungover from the flight and night before. I told myself to not think and just go, and with that, I left my luggage at the front desk and off we went. As we got to the water, there were two men by a little boat waving for us. Once I saw the men and the boat, I realized what I was about to do. I immediately started to get nervous, but I knew there was no turning back.

As we rode out to the spot we were going to dive, one of the guides pulled out a joint and of course, a few of us smoked it. I remember getting pretty high because I hadn't really slept or eaten much in a couple of days. When we finally got to the dive spot, the guides had us jump in the water so we could get used to breathing with the gear on. I remember being really uneasy in the water because of possible sharks and as I floated in the water, I was wondering if there were any around me. While in the water, they had each of us go underwater and practice breathing. Then we got back in the boat and split into two groups. I chose the second group to give me some time to gather myself before I dove. As I was trying to mentally prepare for what I was about to do, the guide passed the joint again and I smoked it. Now I was pretty well cooked and soon it was my time to dive.

As I watched the first group come back and get in the boat I had to kick into a different gear. I tried to just clear my mind and relax. I got in the water and down we went. Not only was this my first-time diving, but I was hungover, tired, hungry, and now really stoned. As we were going down, I could see the sunlight in the water above me, and then all of a sudden we made a turn and it went pitch black. I could only see right in front on me and all I could hear was my heartbeat pounding. The next thing I saw were these little rays of light and the guide was now pointing to my oxygen meter giving me a signal to slow my breathing. As I am starting to try and relax, the guide frantically points to my mask because it was filling up with blood and I didn't even notice it. When he pointed to my mask he then pointed downward, so I looked down and there were brown tip sharks swimming right below me. I then looked at my mask and it was now almost half-filled with blood. I immediately tried to swim to the top but the guide grabbed me and pointed up. So, I looked up and now I saw barracudas swimming above me. I was surrounded by potential death and did not know what to do. The guide was still holding me and took me down around a rock. We just sat for what seemed like forever before he opened my mask to get the blood out. He then hit my oxygen gauge and showed me that I was running out of air—Really!!?? Now I was getting real freaked out, but I was so tired that I could barely swim. The next thing I knew, the guide was taking me around another rock and then finally up to the surface. We came up right next to the boat, and as soon as we surfaced, the guide said something to his partner and he got me in the boat.

Remember, I had never been scuba diving before and when I asked the guide how far down we had gone he showed me the dive meter which was stuck at 30 meters. I had no idea how far down that was and I found out later that it was 100 feet and that diving 100 feet on my first dive was insane. I was later told that the combination of diving 100 feet, not being decompressed from my flight, having no sleep, and all the alcohol, cocaine, and the joint I smoked was a deadly mix and it was a miracle I did not go into cardiac arrest while in the water. When it was time for the next dive, I just sat in the boat exhausted, hungover, hungry, and now had a massive headache. I was not about to go in the water again. I just wanted to get to the hotel to eat and sleep because I had a photo shoot the next day.

The chance I had been waiting for—shooting the Chippendales calendar—was now beginning to be a nightmare for me because I was so tired and so partied out that I did not even care—I just wanted to sleep. By the time I got back to the hotel I was so delirious that I became restless and actually could not sleep because of my worrying about the shoot and how I would look and feel in the morning.

My wake-up call was set for 6:00 a.m. and when it went off, I just laid in bed feeling totally wiped out and upset for not holding off on the partying until after the shoot. By this point I knew how to kick myself into another gear, so I went and had some breakfast and a couple of Bloody Mary's and then found someone with a joint. After that I was once again comfortably numb. As I headed back to my room, I stopped at the front desk to check on any messages and sure enough I had received one informing me that my shoot was moved to the afternoon and evening. What a break that was for me. I was able to eat more, sleep more, and recover on the beach.

By afternoon, I was physically and mentally ready for the shoot, but now they were not ready for me. While I waited in my room, I had a couple more drinks and finished the joint from earlier. When they finally called me for the shoot, I was pretty buzzed. I walked down to the beach and I saw one of the camera crew waving me to a boat which would take us to a remote spot on the island. As we pulled in, I could see the owner, make-up artist, and camera crew waiting for us. As I got off the boat, I remember one of the crew members saying, "Looks like you're feeling pretty good, Kevin."

This was the afternoon shoot, the first of two for me, and when I asked where we were shooting, they pointed out to a towel and a coconut laying on the beach. Then the make-up artist started working on me with powder, mascara, eyeliner and she oiled me up. Next, they had me go out to the towel and get on all fours sprawling out. When the owner saw the test pictures from that pose, he liked it so much he did not move me from that position until he had taken what seemed like hundreds of shots. Then he had me stand up with my backside facing the camera and once again he did not move me. I only posed in those two positions for that segment of the shoot, but that piece took hours. By the time it was done, I was tired, sunburned, and still had the night shoot to go.

When I got back to the hotel, I took a quick power nap, showered, and had room service deliver me some food and a couple drinks before the next part of my shoot. By now I was so ready for the shoot to be over, I just wanted to get on a plane and fly somewhere far away from everyone and everything.

When I got the call, I was told all I had to do was take a little walk out to the beach and I would see a little area with a couple of poles, chairs, and hanging lights. The owner was already there positioning everything as he wanted. This part of the shoot was very easy on me because all I had to do was sit in a chair with a glass in my hand and look drunk. No acting or posing needed for that demand. I just sat there and let them take the pictures. It went very quick and before I knew it, we were done. I remember walking back to my room thinking, *well, it's done!* I was hoping that at least one of the pictures would make it in the calendar.

My flight back to rejoin the tour was the next day and some of the guys were going scuba diving again, the morning before the flight, and of course, I had to try it one more time. When morning came, I had a little breakfast and headed out to the boat. When I got to the boat, it was the same two guides from the day before. They asked if I was okay and if I was sure I wanted to go again. I let them know I was good and ready, so on with the gear and in the water we went. This time we only went down about 40 feet or so, but once again, I had sharks below me and barracuda above me. Before this dive, the guides told us that if the barracuda became aggressive, to put our arms across our chest, grab our shoulders, and not move. This would get them to swim off.

While we were in the water, one of the guys tried to grab the tail of a barracuda. Man, here we go again! The barracuda spun around and in a flash, was facing him, only inches away. I looked around and saw more barracuda moving towards us. As the one barracuda looked at him, we all put our arms in the position we were told and soon after the barracuda swam off. The next issue was that all the commotion from the barracuda stirred up the sharks below us, and at that point, the guides motioned us back to the boat. When we got in the boat, everyone had some explicit things to say to the guy that grabbed the barracuda and I took that as a sign for me to pack it up and head to the airport.

The 1993 Chippendales calendar and the 1993 Chippendales Hot calendar both came out in the summer of 1992. I still remember the night I saw them. I was in London, England performing at the Strand Theatre, and the first show had just ended. I was out back with some of the guys to get some air when another guy walked up to me and asked if I had seen the calendars. I said that I didn't and then asked him why and I will never forget his response. He said, "It is all about you, Kirchen. You are all over both calendars and on the cover of the Hot calendar." When I saw the calendars, I couldn't believe it. Every position I shot made the calendars, and not only did I have a month and a centerfold in the main calendar, but the picture I took sprawled out on the beach towel with the coconut was the cover shot for the Hot calendar.

I did it—I made the calendar and in a big way. I looked at the pictures—it was a bittersweet moment—because I knew I had just accomplished everything there was to accomplish and had told myself many times before that when I made the calendar I was done and I would quit. So, there I was feeling great that I made the calendar, sad because I knew my career was over, and nervous because I didn't know what I would do after I quit.

As I look back, what a crazy time this was. This was just another time that I rolled the dice of life, another time that I didn't really consider what could possibly happen to me, and another time that Almighty God was right there with me. He completely protected me and covered me one more time. His unmerited grace and love for me kept me safe because once again, any of the experiences that happened to me while in Tahiti, whether self-inflicted or not, could have easily killed me. His mercy and grace are so awesome that I have to say again that, "I know it was God and *only* God who brought me back safe and alive."

Once again, I only tell of my time at Chippendales, not to brag or boast, but to show how crazy and uncaring I was. Through all my insane life events, and my threatening and self-gratifying actions, God was with me, protecting me for a time as this.

PORN

I t was the summer of 1992. I had just shot the 1993 Chippendales calendar and returned to join the tour in London. A little while into my return, I was on stage one night performing my act, *Back in Black*, and knew it was time to quit. It was the first time that I had been on stage and felt nothing. I had no excitement, no adrenaline rush, no wanting of women, no anticipation of going out after the show and getting high—I was just numb. Not even the fact that the new calendar had just came out and I was all over it, cover, month, and centerfold could excite me. If there was any time to stay, this was the time, but I just didn't care anymore even though I was about to leave a gang of money on the table. I had nothing left, and I knew it was time to leave or retire, as some might say.

I remember finishing my performance that night and just walking off-stage—no bow, no wave, no thank you. I just walked off. When I got backstage, I quit. I let everyone know I was done and then called the owner to let him know. I was quitting. Yes, it was an eight year run that tried to kill me, and I was burnt out. The traveling, the partying, and performing almost every night finally caught up with me. I had been on the road for over six years with very little time off, because even on my time off, I wasn't resting. I was doing private shows or contests. By the time I decided to quit, I was in a tour fog. I had performed over 4500 shows worldwide for almost two million women. I had been on a non-stop party train. In this stage of my life, I wanted something else. I didn't feel happy. I felt lost and alone, so I thought, *why not try Hollywood?*

When I returned to L.A., I found an agent, or so I thought I did. It turned out the agent was more interested in the fact that I was an ex-Chippendale dancer than anything else. He wanted me to go to clubs with him to promote his agency and help pick up women along the way. I finally got rid of him and was referred to another agent, and now this agent kept trying to hit on me, inviting me to his house, and to weird little parties, which I didn't like going to. So, I got rid of him, also. The whole Hollywood scene I was now involved in was what I had basically just left—the parties, the clubs, the mingling, and the schmoozing. This was the same game I had already been doing for years, so coming home and doing the same thing again just wasn't me anymore. By now I was tired of the clicks, tired of the phony people, tired of the empty promises, and tired of the who's who game. I just wanted to be able to make some good money, slow down, and live my life— whatever that meant.

Then came the night my life took another major turn. I was at a club in Beverly Hills when I saw one of the guys I toured with in Denver years before. He had quit Chippendales and got into the adult movie business. He told me about the business and said I could make a lot of money for having sex. He mentioned that all he did was have sex, party, and get paid, and he said that's what everybody did, so, I could just be me—the party animal. He gave me his agent's number and told me to go see him the next day. I stayed up all night partying into the morning, thinking if I should do it or not, because I knew that once I did a porn scene, I would be a marked man. I knew as soon as I made an adult movie I would be known as a porn star and I was having a hard time absorbing that. I kept running the possible reactions of what people might say when they saw me like, "Aren't you that porn star?" or "Hey, I saw you in that porn movie!" What would I now say when a girl I was interested in asked what I did for work? "Oh, I'm a porn star." I knew my life, my future, and how I would be viewed would completely change if

I made this move. So, after snorting, drinking, and thinking about it—what a great combo, by the way—I decided to give it a shot and go see the agent. Getting paid good money just to have sex and be able to party while doing it began to seem too good to be true.

A couple of days later, I called the agency and made an appointment to meet. I let them know I was referred by one of their actors who I used to work with at Chippendales, and when they heard this they asked me to come in that same day. I didn't know what to expect and was a bit nervous on my way there, so I stopped at a bar and had a couple of shots to kick me into gear. When I arrived, I was greeted by the office manager, and we spoke for a little bit. Then I was introduced to the agent who proceeded to tell me how in demand I would be and how much money I could make per sex scene. I was told I needed to come up with a stage name and then I was asked to strip down nude so they could take some pictures of me. They said the pictures would be put into a booklet, so when producers or talent needed someone for a particular shoot, they could look through this book and choose the actors or actresses from it.

Guy talent and girl talent had separate photo books, and each picture of talent was labeled with different categories of sex scenes each person could perform. The categories were very widespread. Some examples of these categories were straight boy or girl, gay, lesbian, threesomes, orgies, and bondage just to name a few. They also listed what sex acts each person would be willing to do and these I will not list. The number of categories or sex acts you agreed to perform determined how much you worked. The more categories, the more work. The sex acts listed were focused on the girls and so, likewise, the more sex acts the girls were willing to do, the more money they would make. And the dirtier the act, the more the money.

After they took my pictures, I spoke with the agent who asked me to be back at the office the next day to shoot a sex scene for their personal film company. They wanted to see how I would perform in front of a camera, and said it would be a great warm-up for me to get ready for the big time shoots. I was also to come up with a stage name for film– this would be the name I would be known by in the business, they said it had to be something strong and catchy to match my looks. When I showed up the next day for the shoot, I had no idea who I was going to have sex with, and I still didn't have a stage name. For the shoot to happen, we needed a name and we needed it fast. The agent and I got together to figure out a name and after rattling off some names that sounded like typical porn names, the agent and I came up with the name, *Colt Steele*. As I was mulling that name around in my head and practicing introducing myself as *Colt Steele*, a girl showed up to have sex with me. She introduced herself and then said, "I guess I am (explicit) you today." For the first time, I was caught off guard and had no come back or anything to say to that. I was kind of taken back by her matter-of-fact way she introduced herself to me.

From that point on, everything happened very quickly. We were now walking into the room where this scene was to take place and all I was thinking was, *wow, here we go*. This was the moment of no return for me. Once I had sex on camera it would be official. I would be a porn star and the name, *Colt Steele*, would be with me forever. I was always called or introduced as *Colt* and was never called Kevin again until many years later.

The room where we shot the scene was very small and plain. It had a small bed, a nightstand, and some sheets hung on the wall to make it look like a window was there. Before the scene started, the director told us he needed to shoot four different sex positions and then proceeded to tell us the ones he wanted to see. He also told me when, where, and how I was to climax. Once again, I was taken back by the totally nonchalant way that he explained the sex scene to me, and I knew it was definitely just a job and nothing more. You could feel the coldness and pressure as the director was explaining what he wanted. He obviously needed to get the scene done as quickly as possible and with no hiccups.

As the scene progressed, I became very uncomfortable because I was naked with cameras all around me, and I had a lot of things I needed to be aware of, like where the lights were. One wrong move and I could be burned. You had to know where the video cameras were because you couldn't block their view, and if you did, there was explicit language directed towards you. Then you needed to know where the digital camera was because they would ask you to hold positions to find the *look good* shots when they took stills for magazine layouts. You also needed to know where the mic was, so you didn't hit it.

The scene took about two hours to complete and through it all, I had to go to places in my head to get it done. I had to detach myself from the reality of it all and leave my conscious state of mind to go into a fantasy world. I had to tap into places deep inside myself that I had never been before. It really wasn't at all what I expected and it was actually very difficult, but once again I had to show no signs of being nervous or uncomfortable because this shoot was going to either make me or break me. This would be what I was judged on and I had to be good if I was going to work for the big companies.

When the scene ended, I had a bunch of different thoughts and emotions come at me all at once. One of the biggest thoughts was, oh my God, I just became a porn star, and my life is now marked forever. What did I just do? Will I ever have a normal life, now that I did this? But those thoughts were quickly brushed aside for a myriad of thoughts like, *Did she, the actress, like me? Was I now on her request list for actors to work with? Would she tell the other girls they should work with me? How did the agent like me? How was I compared to the other guys? Could I have done better? Was I in good enough shape?* It was a very crazy moment in my mind and in a matter of seconds, I spoke to God saying I was sorry. But then, I completely switched gears and told myself that God was mad. And devil, it was time for you to make me the best male porn actor. How crazy is that!

Before I knew it, everyone had cleaned up, got dressed, packed up, and got ready to go. This experience was very weird for me because everyone just said goodbye to each other like they were at a nine-to-five job and just left. I was amazed at how unattached everyone was. In fact, I remember the director telling the actress he'd like to use her again. That statement basically sums up what the porn industry is all about—using. They will use people until they can use them no more, until they are all used up.

That first scene was the start of a long career in porn, and during that span, I worked with all the big companies. In the beginning, there was this level of excitement about being a porn star. I would walk on sets and see the girls I had watched in movies, and now I was having sex with them. I saw the guys I had watched in movies and wanted to be better than they were. I wanted everyone to know who I was, and I wanted to be famous. In the beginning, shooting a scene was kind of cool and I looked forward to it, but it very quickly became a draining and lonely job. It was a job fueled by public demand, what sex the pubic wanted to see, what sex sold the best, and which actor or actress sold the best. It was and still is about supply and demand with no regard or care for the people doing the scenes. What got the public off is what the porn business produced and if you didn't perform what the business needed, they would find someone who would.

In the beginning I was doing four to five scenes a week, sometimes two a day, and then would go out to party. Once again, I was running myself into the ground—fast—burning the candles at both ends, and not caring about anything but the next high. My time in porn wasn't like my time in Chippendales, however, Sure I partied and had sex with a lot of women at Chippendales, but porn was a very dark, lustful, and damaging business. It had this chemistry that could change anyone over time into the big sex machine that was depressed, addicted, and lost. I watched many girls go from nice to nasty, and not by choice, but because of the industry and its control.

Porn drove me to be this very dark, hidden, and shutdown person. I became more isolated, more lustful, and more reckless. I completely lost myself. My drug, alcohol, and steroid use increased very quickly, I was always on something and always on an emotional rollercoaster. I rarely used heavy drugs or drank on sets because it worked against me and made me shutdown and paranoid. I did, however, on occasion, smoke weed before a shoot, but I even stopped doing that after a while. I always saved my partying for after the shoot because afterward, I had the say of how much and how fast. I figured no one would know my insanity, but eventually everyone knew and word traveled fast.

I performed hundreds of scenes during my time in porn and I saw and experienced a lot of crazy things. One of the craziest things I experienced was having sex with a girl while her boyfriend or husband watched. I even dated girls in the business and the hardest part for me was having your girlfriend leave for work and say something like, "I will be home late. I have three sex scenes today." I even had girlfriends ask me questions like what actor I wanted them to have sex with or if I minded them doing certain things with certain actors. For the most part, the female porn star didn't want their porn star boyfriend to do scenes because they made more money than the guys anyways. I had girls tell me it was better if they worked because they didn't have to get turned on and could fake the orgasm, but a man had to be turned on and had to orgasm and they didn't like that. I even had a girl tell me to promise her I would only think about her while having sex with another woman. This is how crazy and messed up things can be in the porn business, and as I said before, I watched many people change.

I witnessed so many things that I could not believe. I saw girls pass out while having sex as the cameras kept rolling, and girls bleeding, and throwing up while having sex as the cameras kept rolling. I even witnessed producers telling actors and actresses they could not use condoms on their shoots, and if they were set on using one, they would be replaced. I witnessed producers and directors slap girls, and I heard them tell girls to go home and use toys to loosen themselves up so they could handle their next sex scene. I witnessed producers degrade women because of their size or the way they performed acts. And I experienced so many outrageous things, including more drugs and alcohol than I ever had at Chippendales. I saw phony IDs, phony HIV tests, and average, nice, sweet, and innocent people with moral standards change their standards. Their do's and don'ts became why not's for a shot at instant money or the potential of fame and a future payday. I watched as girls were asked to do certain things and when they refused, the producer would offer more money and sometimes continue raising the price until they said yes. Many times, I was given extra money to do shoots I would not normally do.

One of the biggest motivators for girls to compromise themselves was for the opportunity to make big bucks on the strip circuit. Strip clubs and adult book stores will pay a lot of money for porn stars to appear, and at times the dirtier they were on film, the more money they would make. I could go on and on about what I witnessed during my years in porn.

It is only by the grace of God I survived that time and did not become just another name added to the list of porn deaths. See, that's the sad thing. People die in this business and no one really cares—they just find a new actor or actress to fulfill their needs.

I stated during this time, my drug, alcohol, and steroid use became even more profound than at Chippendales. I did everything that was put in front of me, I stayed up for days at a time, I did lethal amounts and lethal combinations, and I was a lost soul who had many battles with depression. Many times, those battles could have ended in an overdose or suicide. At the end of it all, porn had destroyed me and I was so far gone that I didn't care about life or death. But God had a different plan for me, and when I should have OD'd, He covered me. When I entertained thoughts of suicide, He stopped them time and time again. During those times, I still remembered God. I still remembered all those times He had rescued me before, I still remembered that He did love me, and through all my mess and turning away, He was always there and for that I truly give all glory to Him.

To sum it all up, the porn business is a soul feast for the devil—it's all about self-gratification, non-commitment, emotional unattachment, and the idolization of flesh. It's a business of lust, adultery, manipulation, greed, power, and destruction. It allows a false freedom in having casual uninhibited sex with multiple partners, with no commitment and no responsibility for yourself or the other person. It's the devil's playing field and for many of those who decide to go play in it, they eventually lose their choice of how to play or when to quit the game.

At first, porn sounds great to the newcomer who is promised to become a star, and then is offered a lot of money to have a lot of sex and told that they would have the freedom to call their own shots. They are even told it's a great stepping- stone into becoming a mainstream actor or actress. In reality, they are just a piece of meat owned and manipulated by the porn industry, which in turn, is owned and manipulated by the public. The porn industry has no power in and of itself, and they would go broke if the public stopped watching it. Behind the power of porn is the public—the man, woman, or teenager who watches it. What the public desires is what the porn industry delivers, and the performers are just pawns in the supply and demand chess game. Public supply and demand are what truly control the industry. This then dictates the actors/actresses who, what, when, where, and how to have sex. In actuality, nobody cares about the porn star—not the business and not the public.

During my time in the business, I received stacks of fan mail from men, women, married couples, singles, swingers, etc. They would tell me who they liked me working with, what they liked to see, what they wanted to see me do, and who they wanted to see me do it with. By the time I left the business, I was faced with the question of who would ever accept me now—love me or respect me—after what I had done. From my experience, the porn industry usually attracts people who are just looking for acceptance, fame, power, money, fun, or just something in their lives to fulfill an empty hole which only God can fill.

After a while, the game is no longer a game, but a ball and chain that keeps you in it, because your lifestyle now demands you stay in it. When the excitement, money, and popularity is all over, many of the same people are usually worse off mentally and emotionally than when they first decided to play the game.

Porn was an addiction for me that started when I was about 10 years old, looking at my dad's nudie magazines. Who would have thought an innocent curiosity would grow into an addiction to pornographic material that would eventually lead to becoming a porn star. I was a porn actor who got paid for sex and after work, would payout what I made to party and escape, to forget about life and my reality. Sometimes I paid to have more sex after getting paid to have sex—how crazy is that. Porn opened up crazy doors that owned me for a long time. I saw that it owned others, too—it destroyed people's lives, integrity, character, emotions, relationships, friendships, and values, creating isolation, fueling drug and alcohol addictions, ODs, and suicides. Even after quitting the porn business and knowing what I knew about the dark hidden side of porn, I still watched it, until that one day, when God came in and showed me that even though I quit acting in the porn business, I was still a part of the supply and demand chain.

It was a harsh reality realizing that even though I was out of the business, my own need for self-gratification was still fueling the fire for the destruction of others. Today I can say that, through the power of God and the choice to say no, I am completely free from porn.

In closing, please be aware that, if you watch it, read it, or engage in it in any way, you have just entered the devil's game. This is the game he designed to destroy you and your relationships. Porn turns the other person you are with into an object, detaching you from reality, detaching you from true intimacy and commitment, detaching you from your emotions, and detaching you from life. It's a never-ending hamster wheel of fantasy that will never get fulfilled and will always demand more of you. This is what the devil wants—he uses porn as bait to own you, because he wants your life. Think of the devil as the fisherman with the fishing pole. Porn is the bait and the world, you and I, are the fish. And so far, the devil is doing a pretty good job at accomplishing his goal—the goal of destroying what God designed sex to be—a private and intimate time between a husband and wife.

Decades ago, society looked at porn as a dark, underground, nasty, and illegal business, but through the years, it has subtly become a legal, accepted, promoted, advertised, and admired business. I am amazed at the times we are in now, where kids actually want to become porn stars. It's become a career path for our youth. Porn is now cool. We are now all in a society that openly accepts it and even uses it to teach kids about sex. What a great way to slowly destroy the next generation and the intimacy of the marriage bed. The world thinks it's coming up with some very intelligent standards and ideas with teaching our youth, but in reality, it is doing exactly what the devil set out to do from the very beginning—to kill, steal, and destroy.

It is my prayer that everyone stays away from the waters of porn and doesn't take the bait of destruction. Instead, my hope is that people will press towards the enjoyment of what God had designed sex to be—true intimacy shared between a husband and his wife. Sexual intimacy is not found online, in a magazine, on a DVD, in a bar, in a strip club, or on a corner. God designed true sexual intimacy to be experienced only when a husband and wife come together as one.

The great news is this—as with any addiction, you only have to stay away one day at a time, and if you should fall, here is my personal instruction manual:

1. Put it down, shut it down, or walk away.

2. Give it to God, ask for forgiveness, and move on.

3. Find someone you can confide in, who won't judge you, and talk about it together.

4. Find some godly person or people to pray with you and for the chains of addiction to be broken.

5. Repeat if/when needed. Most importantly, don't give up!

I personally fell many times and was a repeat offender. I did steps one to three a lot, but I kept pressing towards the goal of freedom. Then one day, I realized that because of my choices, I hadn't succumbed to the addiction in a while, and that was the day I knew that the addiction had truly been removed and that I *was free*. I became free when I stopped trying to stop and started choosing God, seeking Him in those times of weakness. Evil lives in the dark, so once I became open and honest about myself and truly understood that Jesus did love me just as I was and that the One who knew no sin, became sin for me, I began to believe who I was in Christ. The only thing keeping the addiction around and active was my free will to do and choose whatever I wanted. I could choose life or death, freedom or bondage, an old life or a new life—it was my choice.

Scripture says:

> *Submit therefore to God. Resist the devil and he will flee from you. - James 4:7 (NASB)*

> *No temptation has overtaken you but such as is common to man; and God is faithful, who will not allow you to be tempted beyond what you are able, but with the temptation will provide the way of escape also, so that you will be able to endure it. - 1 Corinthians 10:13 (NASB)*

> *For we do not have a high priest who cannot sympathize with our weakness, but One who has been tempted in all things as we are, yet without sin. Therefore, let us draw near with confidence to the throne of grace, so that we may receive mercy and find grace to help in the time of need. – Hebrews 4:15-16 (NASB)*

Let me add this, and maybe it will help someone understand what Jesus did on the cross when He became sin. Christian or not this is the reality—

Jesus died as: an alcoholic, a drug addict, a murderer, a liar, a thief, a rapist, a violent and abusive person. He died addicted to porn, addicted to sex, an adulterous person, a hypocrite, a cussing, rude, vulgar, hateful person, coveting everything, an idolater, a sexual pervert, a blasphemer, a devil worshiper, a terrorist, an atheist, an agnostic, prideful, arrogant, unloving, etc.

He died depressed, suicidal, broken, and alone. He was an outcast, unwanted, and unloved. He experienced every destructive and self-sabotaging feeling humanly possible and He did it for you, so that through Him, you could truly be set free!

God made Jesus, who knew no sin to be sin on your behalf, so that we might become the righteousness of God in Him (or in right standing relationship). – 2 Corinthians 5:21 (NASB)

And He did it for you! Because He Loves you and wants you to be free!

Jesus answered them, "Truly, truly, I say to you, everyone who commits sin is the slave of sin. The slave does not remain in the house forever; the son does remain forever. So, if the Son makes you free, you will be free indeed!" - John 8:34-36 (NASB)

If He loves me enough to set me completely free, He will set you free, too! The beauty is, all you have to do is truly ask, but once we ask, we have to always choose Him.

Drugs, Alcohol, Steroids,
AND DEATH

The day the calendar came out was the day I decided to quit Chippendales and I told myself I would quit using any mind-altering chemicals, too. Quitting Chippendales was easy, but quitting all the mind-altering chemicals wasn't that easy. I thought I could just quit because Chippendales, the road, and everything that came with it. Right? At the time, however, I couldn't just quit, because somewhere along the way, I crossed the line of me controlling the alcohol and drugs to the alcohol, drugs controlling me.

I remember in the first couple of years working in the L.A. Club, a quarter gram of cocaine would last me a couple of nights. Then that same quarter gram only lasted a few hours. Soon, I started buying a gram of cocaine for the weekends, and then that gram started lasting only one night.

While on tour, finding the cocaine in different cities was challenge because I would have to go to local clubs or bars after our shows and ask people I had just met if they knew where to get it. I really didn't like being in an unfamiliar city asking random people where I could get cocaine, but I had to if I was going to party. It took a minute, but I was able to master different ways of finding who could get me the cocaine without straight up asking.

One night, after one of our shows, I had a few girls ask me and a few of the other guys to party with them – I was all in for partying but I needed some cocaine. I hadn't had any in a few days and I was desperate, so desperate that I did not care who I asked, so when the girls asked to party with us – I said "You can party with us if you can get us some cocaine", I think the guys were kind of shocked that I straight out asked the girls if they could get cocaine, in fact I remember one of the guys saying "it's for him not for me" and to my surprise one of the girls said she could get some. When I heard that I immediately took control of the situation and had her make the call, then I told her if she could get it quick enough we would go to my room and party. She asked how much I wanted and I told her two grams. She made the call and when she came back to me, she said she ordered an eight ball, which is about three and a half grams. She told me it was a better deal for the money and that we had to go right away to pick it up because the guy was about to leave.

This was the first time I had ever asked a random woman from our show if she could get cocaine and it was a pretty crazy thing to do for a few reasons. This girl could have been setting me up, since I didn't know her nor had a clue where we were going. I was also pretty drunk and forgot the name of the hotel we were staying at. In addition to this, I was carrying a bunch of cash and headed to make a drug deal by myself and no one in my group, including me, knew where she was taking me. That one night set the tone for how I would live my life on the road, knowing that I could just ask the girls from our shows to get my cocaine was perfect for me and it became my routine.

Eventually, I started looking for *my cocaine girl* before the first show, and if I couldn't find her, I would look for her after the first show. If I still didn't find her, I would look again before the second show and at the after party. Once I found her, I would convince her to get the cocaine as soon as possible. Sometimes she would go during the show to get it, or even completely miss the show to secure some. Looking back, some of these women weren't even inside the venue yet, they hadn't even had any drinks, and they were just waiting in line to get in. When I did find the girl who could and would get the cocaine, I was giving her a lot of cash and only hoped that she would come back with the cocaine, or at least come back with my money. I must say, in all my times of just giving a girl money to go get cocaine, I was never ripped off and I can count on one hand how many times a girl came back with the money and not the cocaine. It didn't matter what town, what city, what state, what providence, or what country I was in. I almost always found the girl who knew where to get cocaine. There were only two reasons I didn't get cocaine. This was because we were either in a small town that was dead to partying, or I wasn't looking because I was so burnt out that I needed to shut it down for a night.

In the beginning, my party runs looked something like this—one Bacardi and Coke before the first show and another after the show. Then, I would have another two to three drinks at the after party and a half gram to one gram of cocaine to cap it off. I could usually keep this pace up for three or four nights in a row. By the time I had reached my second year on tour, my party runs looked something like this—a few Bacardi and Cokes before the first show and another one backstage during the show. Then, after the first show, I would head to the hotel bar and have one or two more to get ready for the second show. During the second show, I would have a drink and after the show, I would head over to the hotel bar again or a local club to finish the party. I was doing two to three grams of cocaine a night and doing it four to five nights a week.

At my peak, I was doing no less than an eight ball of cocaine almost every night. I partied a solid five to six night a week. I always had to have cocaine. The anticipation of doing cocaine consumed me to the point of it being all I thought about as I traveled from place to place. I was so out-of-control that I was constantly partying, even on the bus, as we headed to the next town while everyone else slept. On occasion, I even did cocaine in-between shows and during shows. I continued partying when I was sick and with a fever. Cocaine had me in its grip so much so that if I didn't have it, I felt lonely and depressed. I was now chasing the cocaine, so I could be social and chasing after party sex, so I wouldn't be alone. No cocaine meant no sex, and no sex meant I would be alone—so, getting cocaine was a must.

Another occurrence during my first year on tour, was that I was introduced to steroids and quickly found that by using them, I could keep my edge. I remember the first time I was asked to go in on a cycle—I had no idea what that meant, what it would do to me, or how it would make me feel. I asked some questions about it and was told it would make me big, strong, and I would always be in shape. When I heard this, I was all in.

The first steroid cycle I took was Winstrol and Deca Durabolin. I still remember the first time I shot myself with it. I was very nervous as the needle was going in and all I could do was hope I wouldn't have a heart attack. My first cycle lasted eight weeks and I was told I should not drink alcohol or do cocaine because I could have a reaction to it. Not drinking or doing cocaine only lasted until I pushed the envelope and did it anyway. I remember having a drink and feeling this rush, and then I did a small line of cocaine to make sure I would be ok. Once I saw that I survived, I went for it and did a bigger line, which gave me this huge rush, and I could actually feel my body temperament changing.

By my second year on tour, my steroid consumption changed, and I found myself not only going over the recommended dosage, but I was also staying on the cycles longer. I never considered myself addicted to steroids because I only related addiction to drugs and alcohol, but as you will see, I was addicted to steroids, also. An 8-week cycle now became 12, and a 12-week cycle became 16. I actually stopped counting weeks and I just stayed on until the bottles were empty. I was not starting my cycles off slowly, peaking in the middle, and tapering them down as I was told to. When I was on, I was on, and I started the cycle and finished the cycle the same way—full steam ahead. I was just as excited and consumed by steroids as I was by cocaine, and I became completely unsettled and even angry when I was out of steroids. In fact, I relied on them so much I was ordering more cycles before I was through with what I had. The only time I was off a cycle was when I couldn't find it in the city I was in, or I couldn't get it sent out to where I was.

By my third year, I was doing to two to four cc's a week and combining one to three different steroids at one time, both oral and injectable. Not only was I hitting my steroid use hard, but I was still doing my eight balls of cocaine and drinking on top of that. I was so crazy in my use of steroids that I would sometimes even double-up on the shots or the pills the morning after a long night of partying to make sure I would have a pump for the show that night. If I missed a shot, I would look at myself thinking I was losing weight or getting small and I hated that feeling. So, I would always carry an oral supply with me at all times, just in case I didn't make it back to the hotel in time to take my shot. I traveled from city to city, state to state, country to country, and to other continents and I always had it on me. Through airport terminal check points, bus terminal check points, customs check points, border patrol check points, it didn't matter what the check point was, I just went through them like it was no big deal.

There are many different kinds of anabolic steroids of which I used 13 of them. Here is a list of the steroids I used—Anadrol, Anavar, Clenbuterol, Deca Durabolin, Dianabol, Equipoise, Human Growth Hormone, Primobolan, Sustanon, Cypionate, Testosterone Suspension, Sustanon 250, and Winstrol – V.

While writing this chapter, I felt it important to show what I did, how much I did, and how long I did it for. I want to give you an idea of how much cocaine, alcohol, and steroids I put into my body during my career at Chippendales and I hope you see that the grace and mercy of God and His purpose for my life is the only reason I am still here to tell you about it.

I performed over 4,500 shows, averaging two shows per night, which breaks down to 2,225 nights that I did shows. I drank before and after every show and I consumed at least two to three grams of cocaine almost every night. Subtracting sick time, travel time, and the times I could not find cocaine, let's take the 2,225 nights down to 2,000 times I did cocaine while at Chippendales. Now let's add the 2,000 times to the two to three grams I did each in those times—that totals 4000 to 6000 grams of cocaine. One kilo of cocaine is 1000 grams and one kilo or 1000 grams has a weight of 2.2 pounds, so this means I consumed between 8.8 and 13.2 pounds of cocaine or roughly 4 to 6 kilos during my Chippendales career.

Now, let's bring my steroids use during Chippendales into the picture. There are 52 weeks in a year and I was on tour about 6 years. 52 x 6 = 312 weeks. Subtracting the times I was out of steroids or couldn't find them, let's take the 312 weeks down to 250 weeks that I was on steroids while at Chippendales. Now, let's add the 250 weeks to the 2-4 cc's I did each of those weeks, and that totals 500 – 1000 cc's. Now add the combination of one to three different steroids I stacked and you have between 500 – 1500 cc's of steroids. 500 cc's is equal to 16.9 fluid ounces and 1500 cc's is equal to 50.72 fluid ounces and this is the total amount of steroids I put into my body during my Chippendales career.

In the multiple years on the road with Chippendales, my estimation of alcohol consumption is uncalculatable, because I drank gallons of alcohol during that span. I also snorted four to six kilos of cocaine and used 500 to 1500 cc's of anabolic steroids. There were also many times that I combined all three of them at the same time, having a few shots of whiskey, then snorting a half gram to a gram line of cocaine, and then shooting multiple cc's of steroids into my body to see what would happen. At this time of my life, I was unsettled and tired—tired of being unhappy, unsatisfied, and unloved and I really didn't care if I lived or died. After I put all three of these substances into my body, I would look up, raise my hands to the heavens and say "Come on! Bring it on!" I just wanted something to happen and I was basically challenging death. To this day, I thank God that the challenge was never fulfilled, and there were many times it could have been. There certainly were times that my body completely shut down and I physically collapsed, only for me to regather myself and continue to party. There were times I picked up the phone to call for help, because I thought I was going to have a heart attack or pass out, only for me to regather myself and continue to party. I had many warnings and many scary moments that should have pushed me to quit, but every time I survived, I forgot how bad it was and did it all over again.

After I quit Chippendales, I moved straight into porn and in porn, my addictions became even stronger and more noticeable, because I was now in one place, the San Fernando Valley. I was working when I wanted to work or needed to work, which meant I could go on longer runs, and two to three day runs became my norm. During my time in porn, I started to smoke the cocaine rather than snort it, and I also started to smoke meth and glass. I did ecstasy, acid, and even smoked heroine a few times. I was completely hooked and needed to be high or buzzed to socialize in any way. My drug of choice was still cocaine and by this point, getting high was my only agenda. I was now ordering my cocaine and steroids before I had the money to pay for them, knowing once I finished my sex scenes, I would have the money. I was spending my money as fast as I was making it.

While in the porn business, I partied harder than when I was at Chippendales because I really had no responsibility to be anywhere at any time. I could very easily just disappear into a cocaine and alcohol fog without anyone finding me. I was doing a lot of multiple day runs, sometimes with no sleep and no food, and would still do steroids even in that condition. I remember one infamous steroid run, while in porn, where I was combining Human Growth Hormones with Sustanon 250. I was able to get the Human Growth Hormone prescribed to me because of arthritis and being impotent. The arthritis was a real condition, but impotency, really? I was a porn star, but my arthritic condition wasn't enough to allow the Human Growth Hormone script, so when the doctor told me I was impotent I said "What! No, I am not. I am definitely not impotent."

The doctor just shook his head and said, "Yes, you are, if you want this HGH, then you are impotent."

I caught on and said, "Yes, yes I am impotent and I need some help to fix that!" And that was how I got my prescription for Human Growth

Hormone. Once I started this cycle, I was injecting both Human Growth Hormone and Sustanon 250 into my body two to three times a week for over six months and was only directed to do the drugs one to two times per week for three months.

During this run was the first time I tried crack cocaine. It all started with me getting a room at this certain hotel, because it was very close to my dealer's place. I started going to this hotel when I saw prostitutes going in and coming out of it and after seeing that, I knew it was the perfect place for me to party. So, on this particular night, I needed to get a room because I had a large amount of cocaine and was too high to drive. As I was walking to my room, I saw a female coming down the hallway, and she asked if I needed some company. I said, "Yes. Come to my room in a few of hours." When she showed up, I was almost out of my cocaine and asked if she knew where to get some more. I needed her to get it because I was too high to go back to my dealer.

She said, "I can get you something better that will rock your world." I was all in when I heard this and asked what she had. She pulled out a pipe and said, "Here, hit this." That was it for me. Once I smoked my first hit of crack, I never went back to snorting cocaine again. I kept going back to that hotel to party and would be there for days getting high. During one of my runs at that hotel, I was introduced to a drug called *glass*. This was the first time I smoked this. I had no idea what would happen and I smoked so much so fast that I was up for five days. It was such a hard high and come down that I only smoked it if I couldn't find crack. My addiction to smoking crack was so much stronger than anything I had ever battled and it became my drug of choice because I could no longer snort drugs anymore. Snorting any drugs now made my left eye water and burn because the drugs were actually coming out of my eye, but that didn't stop me from snorting if I really had to. I would snort the drug, grab my eye in pain, and wait until I was ok and go at it again.

My time in porn was completely out of control. I was doing more drugs than ever and having more sex than ever. I was either getting high, having sex, coming down, sleeping, recovering, or doing something to be able to buy more cocaine. I definitely became careless with who I was getting my drugs from, who I was hanging with, where I was hanging out, and how much I was doing. I was smoking hundreds of dollars of crack per run, and I would smoke so hard and so fast that there were a few times that the dealers would not sell me anymore. They told me they didn't want me to die. Now when a dealer who makes his money selling drugs says no to you, even when you offer to pay more than the street price, you know you must be in a severely bad spot. I will not even try to calculate how much cocaine I snorted, how much crack I smoked, and how many steroids I did during my time in porn because as I stated earlier, I was completely out of control. It would also be impossible to calculate the glass I smoked that one time, the meth I smoked, or the speed I did while in porn. To get the best and easiest picture of my total drug, alcohol, and steroid use over my porn years, we can just double the use from my time with Chippendales.

The total usage of cocaine, alcohol, and steroid during the years at Chippendales would look like this:

- 4,000 – 6,000 grams or 8.8 – 13.2 pounds of cocaine

- 500 cc's – 1500 cc's or 16.9 – 50.72 fluid ounces of steroids

Let's double the amount I used at Chippendales to cover for the years of partying in the porn industry. The total would look something like this:

- 8,000 – 12,000 grams or 17.6 – 26.4 pounds of cocaine

- 1000 cc's – 3,000 cc's or 33.8 – 101.44 fluid ounces of steroids

- Uncalculatable gallons of alcohol

I would like to tell you that my usage stopped there, but it continued off and on. During this time, I had many bouts of sobriety and clean time, too. During this time, I also had many close calls when my breathing stopped or I was physically paralyzed from days of not eating and barely drinking.

I distinctly remember one morning in December at about 3 a.m., I was in my room laying on my bed watching TV, feeling a little tired from all the partying I had done the day before. My body started feeling funny, my breathing was off, and I got really hot, so I sat on the edge of my bed to try and gather myself when a big dark image moved from the bedroom door towards me. This image swirled in a smoke- type shape and came to a stop right in front of me, forming into three separate figures. When these figures got in front of me, they each raised their arms in a slow swooping motion and moved towards me. I knew it was death coming to get me and I cried out to God, "No God, not now, please! Not now, I want to live!" After that plea, the images broke up into little pieces, scattered towards the ceiling, and disappeared. I knew I was knocking on deaths door with all my drug use and that this experience was a warning as to what was about to transpire if I didn't change my ways. I had been warned many times about my drug use. I had been told I should not be alive. I had been in numerous rehabs and recovery homes and still ignored all of that telling myself I could still do things recreationally and be okay. Now, as I look back, I know it wasn't me telling myself I was going to be okay. It was the devil putting those ideas in my head and me biting on the lie that I could do it one more time. How many times did I bite on that one-more-time lie? Every time!

Scripture says: *Be of sober spirit, be on alert. Your advisory, the devil, prowls around like a roaring lion, seeking someone to devour.* - *1 Peter 5:8 (NASB)*

I did not write about all the cocaine, alcohol, or steroids I did in my life to brag or boast, but to reveal to you how I allowed the devil to try and take me out. Every chemical I used was to either escape a situation, escape a feeling, or to try and make myself become something other than me. I was an empty shell searching for happiness. I just wanted to be accepted, wanted, needed, loved, and not betrayed. The cocaine, alcohol, and steroids never betrayed me, and I knew exactly what I would feel like and I knew I would be comfortable numb. The higher I was and the further from reality I was, the better I felt. I was speeding very fast towards destruction down a highway I could not exit, and the devil tried to keep me right there on it. But God had a different plan.

> Scripture says: *As for you, you meant evil against me, but God meant it for good in order to bring about this present outcome, that many people would be kept alive. – Deuteronomy 50:20 (AMP)*

I will say this, and say it over and over again. It is only by the mercy and grace of God that I am alive today. I have either witnessed or heard of many people who died or became permanently damaged from alcohol, drugs, and steroids. Addiction doesn't care who you are, what you have, or who you know, it's just out to kill. Some people I knew consumed much less drugs than I did but, they died. This confirms the divine presence and loving hand of God on my life. The only thing I did was I never gave up and every time I fell, I got back up. I would fall and cry out to God because I just wanted it all to stop. He heard every cry, He wiped every tear, He helped me get back up every time I fell, and He used all the pain, all the defeats, all the loneliness, and all my desperation for His Glory. He is why I am writing this book, He is the one that made me for a time as this, He is the one who I owe my whole being to. He never left me, never forgot me, and never ignored my cries for help. Instead He kept me, covered me, and protected me for a time such as this.

Some who read this chapter might think it was just luck that I survived, but as we all know, luck runs out. If you compare luck to water in a glass, when you pour the water out, all you have is an empty glass. No more water = No more luck. So, if you are talking luck, I will say this—luck ends it runs out—but God will never end or run out because God is God and He has the final say on everything.

For anyone reading this chapter who is still going through the fire of addiction, please do not give up—but *get up*. Get up and know that God has got you. He is in it with you and your testimony is being made in the fire. Whatever you are going through or have been through, is for someone else. Your story and your victory is someone else's hope.

Scriptures says: *No temptation has overtaken you such as is common to man; and God is faithful, who will not allow you to be tempted beyond what you are able, but with the temptation will provide the way of escape also, so that you will be able to endure it.* – *1 Corinthians 10:13 (NASB)*

The Lord is the one who goes ahead of you; He will be with you. He will not fail you or forsake you. Do not fear or be dismayed. – *Deuteronomy 31:8 (AMP)*

For me, the real fight was staying in the fight and never giving up. No matter who or what I had in my life, no matter what I had experienced in my life, I still felt alone, and unfulfilled. I finally had to completely trust in God for everything and I had to completely surrender my life to Him, and in completely surrendering my life to God, I have experienced complete victory from my old life and the past.

Scripture says: *Therefore if anyone is in Christ, he is a new creature, the old things passed away; behold, new things have come.* - *2 Corinthians 5:17 (NASB)*

Scripture also says: *If anyone wishes to come after Me, he must deny himself, and take up his cross and follow Me. For whoever wishes to save his life will lose it; but whoever loses his life for My sake will find it.* - *Matthew 16:24-25 (NASB)*

Depression, Anger, and
THOUGHTS OF
SUICIDE

T he battles with depression, anger, and thoughts of suicide started when I was 12 years old, after my father died. This continued off and on for decades.

I was taught at a very young age, that I couldn't show any emotions and if I did, I had to shut it down and bury it because it was a sign of weakness. I was always told that men don't show emotion, and that men don't cry. So anytime I was sad, hurt, or just felt like crying, I couldn't. I had to be tough and push the emotion down so I wouldn't look like a sissy, according to my dad.

I was just 12 years old when my mom told me my dad wouldn't be coming home because he died. When she told me, I was devastated. I remember my heart just sank and I didn't know what to think. I cried for a few minutes and then shut it down. Later that day, I cried when I was alone in my room, wondering why this happened to me, and soon after that came the day when I would start to cry and then out of nowhere, I would just stop. I automatically shut down. I never openly mourned the loss of my dad in any way, in fact, I didn't even cry at his funeral. When my dad died, I had all kinds of feelings going on inside of me. Feelings of abandonment, loneliness, confusion, sadness, anger, and fear.

Then came the molestation I experienced by my babysitter. I endured this a few times before and after my dad's death. My mom really liked this person a lot, and I never figured out why. My dad, on the other hand, was always against the babysitter thing and many times my mom and dad would argue about the issue. My dad felt I was old enough to stay home by myself. He would always tease me by saying things like, "Oh, look! The little boy needs a babysitter, how cute." Then he would let me know that babysitters were for *sissys* and since I was letting mom get a babysitter for me, I must be a sissy. So naturally, when this babysitter started molesting me, I felt like I had no one to talk to. I certainly couldn't tell my dad for fear of what he might say or do, and I couldn't tell my mom because she wouldn't believe me.

The whole experience was crazy for me because I didn't know what to do and felt I couldn't tell anyone. While these things were happening to me, I had all these feelings and emotions that would come up inside of me and the worst thing was the feeling of no escape. Not knowing what to do, I had to completely shut down and remained silent about what was happening and that allowed this babysitter to just keep on molesting me. After my dad died, the molestations continued and I still didn't know how to stop it from happening. I was ashamed of what was happening to me, because I knew it wasn't right, and I sure didn't want anyone ever finding out.

One evening, my mom asked me to call for the babysitter to come over. I was in shock that she asked me to call and I knew I didn't want this person coming over, so, I waited to make the call. I waited so long that there was eventually no time left for the babysitter to come over, and my mom was forced to let me stay by myself. That was it, finally, after all this time, I got my chance to escape the torment. That was the first night she ever asked me to make the phone call, and the last time I was ever molested.

I was just 14 years old when my mother chose her boyfriend over me. I couldn't figure out why my mom decided to drive me to the police station and file a police report stating I was an incorrigible runaway. Sadly, the police told her to say this if she didn't want me anymore. I don't know how she could just drive off and leave me there without saying anything. I remember watching her drive away from the station while the police were holding me. I was very sad and confused, and I remember the feeling I had inside of me. The feeling of being hollow and dead. My life seemed pretty much over. It was completely turned upside-down, and in less than two years, both parents were now out of my life—one dead and the other one kicking me to the curb.

Now what I am about to say might sound a bit harsh, but it's my truth.

As I look back now, I believe it would have been easier for me to deal with my mom's death, than to deal with her choice of betrayal and total abandonment towards me.

Fast forwarding ahead, I was just 17 years old when my foster family asked me to leave, and by this time, I had experienced so many bad things in my life that when this happened, I went into a complete emotional shutdown. Why? Well, by now, I had been rejected, betrayed, abandon, used, and abused so much that I told myself I could trust no one and nothing. All I ever wanted as a kid was to be loved and accepted like all of my other friends, but that just didn't seem to be the case for me. So now, I had to find something, or someone to fill that void.

As I moved on in life, the emotional shutdown never left. It triggered anger and depression which lead to some very crazy behavior. Eventually anger and depression became my closest companions and both had the power to overwhelm and control me at any given moment. These two emotions were very strong and powerful and when they rose up, I would either go off on my own or shut down completely. I quickly found that I could best manage my depression with isolation and sleep, but my anger was a different story. I had zero control of it. At times, it was such a raging type of anger that, when it rose up, it even scared me. With the rage sometimes scaring me I then added passivity to my emotional collection. Passivity was a real beast, because I would let things happen or allow people to say or do certain things, because I was afraid of myself and what I knew I was capable of. In these moments of being passive, I found the only way I knew that would protect them and me. Later on, I found that I could sometimes control this rollercoaster of emotions by getting really loaded off some kind of mind- altering substance. Once I did this, I was moved into an uncaring state and completely felt numb.

Eventually, as time went on, the sleep didn't help the depression any longer and the mind-altering substances didn't help control the anger. This put me in a volatile emotional typhoon that could react at any moment. Many times, these emotions had me feeling as though I had no way out, and I felt completely boxed- in and I couldn't even think straight. Many times, I felt as though reality was nowhere in sight and calmness was unattainable. These times made me feel so completely crazy and so overwhelmed that I just wanted my head to stop, to get silent, but I couldn't get my mind to do this. There were many times I would just sit alone with my elbows on my knees and rock or drag my hands through my hair over and over again. Or, I would pace back and forth in one spot. Depending on how bad I was, I could also bang my head on the wall or even destroy things. It was basically anger and passivity at its finest.

When I was a bit older, there came a day when the feelings of anger, depression, loneliness, passivity, and failure became so bad that I decided I didn't want to live anymore. My Chippendales career had already ended and my porn career was in full swing. I was completely lost at this point in my life and didn't like anything or anyone, including myself. It seemed as though I was always alone, when in fact I wasn't. I was just so detached and so self-absorbed that no matter how big or small the crowd was, I felt alone. I burned through many relationships and left many people in the dust wondering what happened. By now, these thoughts of depression, anger, and suicide became so strong that I started to think about truly ending it all. The voices I heard, the thoughts I had, and the feelings I felt would rise up with no warning and sometimes with no reason. I could be completely happy one minute and out of nowhere, get in some funk that would trigger either depression or anger. There were times I would unconsciously look back on my past mistakes, decisions, or the having-no-family issue, and think of suicide. So many times, I just didn't want to live anymore.

I will never forget one afternoon, sitting in my house, with a loaded 9mm in my hand. I was just coming down from a huge cocaine run and had this overwhelming feeling that I would never be able to stop getting high. I would never be accepted by anyone and I would never ever be happy. As I sat in this chair, I kept putting the clip in the gun and then taking it out. I did this three or four times, thinking about life and how it sucked, and then I put the clip back in the gun one more time, and this time I left it in. I pulled the slide back on top of the barrel to load the chamber and let it go, and now the gun was fully loaded and I was ready.

For some reason, at that moment, I held the gun, looked at it for a minute and then decided to put the barrel of the gun in my mouth. When I put the barrel of the gun in my mouth, I had all the intentions of pulling the trigger, but then the craziest thing happened. I started thinking about where I would end up after it was all over—meaning heaven or hell. Then, I heard this very loud voice say, "I love you, and I need you to live. If you do this, he will win and it will be all over." When I heard this, I took the gun out of my mouth and looked to see who was there and nobody was around. I was all by myself.

I know now that voice was the voice of God that spoke and woke me up. Had I pulled the trigger that day, the devil would have won. The devil wanted me to end it all that day— he wanted me to think I was beyond help and that I was hopeless. He wanted me to pull the trigger and end it, and if I had, he would have won—but, I didn't and he didn't win. Praise God!

What is so amazing, is that, for one brief moment, all the voices and confusion going on in my head stopped, and that's when God spoke.

It was in that brief moment of silence and peace, when God gave me the choice to choose life or death. It was in that brief moment that the devil tried to take me out and God said no way, not now. It wasn't until much later that I realized what I was about to do that day was a permanent solution to a temporary problem. It was a solution that would have ended my story and my testimony of who God is.

Some of my worst depression, anger, or thoughts of suicide came either before or after a long run of getting high. These emotions were always directed at something or someone and most of the time that someone was me. I got high to either escape a memory, a situation, or a supposed problem and when these thoughts came, they were always followed by the tormenting thought of destruction. I was so deep in my addictions and so unwilling to stop because at the time, and in those moments, I knew nothing else. I hated being in my own skin, especially my sober skin, and I couldn't imagine ever being able to let the past go. I had no idea that my continued pain was self-induced because I was listening to the wrong voice—the voice of death and destruction.

It wasn't until later on in life that I realized how much of my life I had spent trying to bury the past hurts with drugs, alcohol, sex, and isolation. I had held on to these hurts for so long that they actually became my poison. I allowed this poison to run my life, and I allowed it to control me so much that I ruined many relationships, friendships, and opportunities. I allowed this because the old familiar ways of holding on and wallowing seemed easier that truly acknowledging what happened, dealing with the hurt, moving on, and forgiving those involved.

Today, I am a different person. I have worked through those hurts and understand that what happened is just that—what happened. It's my story and how I decide to let it affect myself and others around me, is up to me. Today, I do not have thoughts of suicide anymore and depression doesn't rule me. Thanks to God, I am of a sound mind. As far as my anger goes—well, that is still a choice. I can either choose to hold on to anger, let it fester, and eventually blow up, or I can choose to surrender my choice to be angry, let it go, and give it to God. Sometimes the *letting it go* part is easier said than done, but the more I practiced letting things go and letting God handle things, the easier it was the next time and the more peaceful I became.

A few nuggets that helped me process all my hurts from childhood and even in my daily life now, include understanding that most people only do what's familiar. Issues related to how they were raised, what they saw, how they learned to cope, and what they've experienced, whether good or bad, is sometimes exactly what will show through them.

This makes the statement, "Hurt people hurt people" so true!

Since I have come to know God and have a relationship with Him, I have been able to accept myself and love myself for who God made me to be. I have not allowed those voices to control me. When they try to pop up, I will say something like, "Not today devil. I command you to leave in the name of Jesus." After that, I put God's word to work and confess who I am in Christ.

Scripture says: We are destroying speculations and every lofty thing raised up against the knowledge of God, and we are taking every thought captive to the obedience of Christ. - 2 Corinthians 10:5 (NASB)

Scripture also says: Finally, brethren, whatever is true, whatever is honorable, whatever is right, whatever is pure, whatever is lovely, whatever is of good repute, if there is any excellence and if anything worthy of praise, dwell on these things. - Philippians 4:8 (NASB)

Who I am in Christ means that I have to die to self. I can't be in Christ and be in myself at the same time. Every day, every moment, and even every second, I have to choose to let my pride and ego die and when this happens, I no longer live, but Christ lives in me.

I was one of those people who had accepted Christ, but had no idea what that meant for me. I had no idea what this new life was and who

I was. If you have accepted Jesus Christ into your life and still are not sure who you are in Christ as I was, I would like you to read Galatians, Ephesians, Philippians, and Colossians. These books will help you understand and grasp who we are in Christ.

MY GAME

MY PAIN | MY PURPOSE

THE WHYS

God had a plan for my life from the very beginning and I didn't even know it.

Everyone has Whys in their life. Why did this or that happen or why didn't this or that happen? Many times, throughout my life, I asked myself those questions. This chapter is about the Whys that I experienced in my life, which I believe are now being revealed to me by God. One person may have things happen to them that another may not, but everything happens for a reason, meaning absolutely nothing happens by accident or mistake. Let's not forget the fact that sometimes it's just life that happens, but how we deal with life and its everyday trials, well, that's up to us.

I had some major Whys in my life that I allowed to influence the choices I made and the choices I made influenced the path my life took early on. But God knew exactly what I would do. He knew the choices I would make and the path I would take and the things that would happen, but none of those things could separate me from God's love, mercy, and grace. Looking back at all those choices I made and the different paths I took, God used them all for His glory and a testimony of who He is in my life today.

The devil tried to destroy me. He knew the purpose of my life and what I was destined for, and that's why he paid me a visit at 17 years old. He lured me, and I took the bait. I made the deal thinking my life would change and I would be something big. Oh, how wrong I was. The devil tried to destroy me and by trying to destroy me, he created my story, a story that now allows me to tell you about God. Ha! Ha! Sorry, devil!

Hopefully, as you read about my Whys, it will open your heart to see that God is love and His ways are not our ways. His plans are not our plans. When God showed me the reasons behind my Whys, it made my love for Him so much more and it showed me that He really is love. I really was His child and He really was my Father. God had His eye on me the whole time and walked me though everything all for His glory. He brought me out on the other side, unscathed, and able to tell others about His love.

Why, at the age of 12, did my father die?

I thought this was unfair, since I was just a kid. I thought God was mean and He ruined my life. I was all alone now. My dad, best friend, protector, and baseball coach, was everything to me and now, he was gone. He went in for a second open heart surgery, and I remember being in his hospital room the night before the surgery, laughing and joking with him. I had no idea that this would be the last time we would spend together. I really didn't know how bad he was, until I was later told by my mom that he had been given a choice to either have the surgery and probably live a few months longer, or not have the surgery and maybe not live another day.

Why a second surgery?

Well, because he did not take care of himself after his first open heart surgery. My dad kept smoking and eating really badly, even after the doctors told him to change his ways. The first surgery went so well that he should have not needed a second. The doctors were completely shocked that his arteries had closed up again, since the first procedure should have taken him well into old age, but it didn't. During the second surgery, he died on the table at the age of 48.

I remember going back to school, after the funeral, and I felt like I was an outcast. All my friends looked at me differently, and even my mom was different. I had nobody to teach me anything, nobody to joke and laugh with, nobody to go to games with, nobody to play catch with, and a short time after that, my half-brothers and sister from my dad's side stopped calling or coming by. Everything I knew, everything that made me happy, and all my dreams were gone. It happened so quickly. One minute, I was a happy boy with a mom and dad, and to suddenly have it all stripped away from me that fourth day of November, in 1976, was devastating.

Why, at the age of 14, was I homeless and on the streets?

I couldn't believe this was really happening. I was just a kid. All the other kids were at home with their families, having fun playing, eating food, watching television, and basically doing whatever families do, but I was on the streets. How did this happen? What did I do to deserve this? It had only been a little over a year since my dad had died, and now my mom was kicking me out. She basically traded me for her new boyfriend.

I still remember the day it happened. My mom's boyfriend had stopped by our house after his normal daily bar time. His routine was to get off work and go to the local bar, and sometimes he would call our house and invite my mom to come out and drink with him. Or, if his other women were at the bar, he would stop by afterwards to chill out a bit before he drove home. One day, he came by after the bar, and he had been drinking a bit more than usual. My mom and I were talking about my dad and he butted in and started talking badly about my dad, saying my dad was no good, and that he had known my dad from work and didn't like him. Listening to this made me angry and I asked my mom if she was going to stand there and let him talk about my dad like that. She just looked at me and said nothing. At that point, I called her boyfriend some explicit names and challenged him to step outside. I was just a kid and he was over 50, but that didn't matter. I was angry and I was going to defend my dad.

We got outside and he asked what I was going to do. I said nothing, I just walked up to him and punched him right in the face, knocking off his glasses. About that time, my mom came outside. You would have thought she would have done something to stop this situation, like tell her boyfriend he was wrong or maybe defend me, but she did nothing. She didn't even come outside with me when I challenged him. She just sat in the house complaining that the neighbors would get upset. When she finally came outside, her boyfriend said, "Look what your boy did! He's crazy." Then he told her it was him or me and the rest is history. I was out.

She called the police on me and told them I hit her boyfriend and that I was uncontrollable. Next thing I know, she was driving me to the police station and filing a report on me. I was handcuffed and put in a cell with other runaways. In the cell were two other guys and a girl, and one of the guys said he had a car a few blocks away and that we should all bust out and get to his car and just disappear. I was okay with that and so were the others, so we busted out of jail through a window and made our way to his car. He asked us all to pool any money we had together, so we could get some alcohol, and we did. We stopped at a liquor store, got some alcohol, and we just sat in the car in the parking lot and drank. Soon after that, I noticed we were all completely drunk and that I couldn't even focus.

We started to drive off and all of a sudden, the driver became angry. Then, he started to cuss about the police, about what happened to him, and then hit the accelerator. In a flash, I realize we are flying down streets, weaving in and out of traffic. We were running red lights, driving on the wrong side of the road, and going over 100 mph. The next thing I know, we have police cars chasing us, and even a helicopter flying over our car. Then we started yelling at this guy to pull over, but he wouldn't.

He just kept going, and after almost crashing, he decided then to pull over. When we pulled over the police had their guns pointed at us while they pulled the driver out of the car and handcuffed him. They had each of us get out of the car, one at a time, and they didn't handcuff or arrest the rest of us. They just put us into a separate car and drove us back to the police station.

It was a short time after that, when I was released back to my mom, who then had me go to L.A. to stay with her other son who was my half-brother. But this brother did not let me stay with him, because his wife said no. So, I ended up couch surfing around L.A., until I eventually meant my foster family.

It wasn't until much later in my life, after Chippendales and after porn, that I was baptized a second time and I really decided to seek God. I wanted to question God and ask why everything happened to me the way it did. When I finally got quiet and really listened, He revealed the answers to me.

Through my seeking and asking, God showed me that my dad's death was inevitable and that everything I went through had to happen. It was all needed for me to get where I am now. Some may think this sounds crazy, crazy that God allowed my dad to die when I was 12, crazy that God would allow me to be homeless at 14 and again at 17, and crazy that I would be molested and eventually find myself drowning in addictions. But it all happened, and He knew I would be strong enough to make it through all that mess, and that I would eventually tell others about Him and what He did for me.

Why did my dad die?

I believe this was because I worshiped him so much and I wanted to be just like him so badly that I would have missed or refused the opportunity to accept Jesus into my life. See, my dad was Catholic, and my mom was whatever-fit-at-that-time, so our family was Catholic. I was raised on go to church on Sundays, say a prayer, go to confession, and that was it. I had never seen a Bible, heard about Jesus, or even God for that matter. I was raised to know that God was mean, Jesus was for freaks, and if you messed up, you would be punished and go to hell.

I grew up knowing that Sunday was the day you went to church, because you had to, and if you didn't, you were going to hell. After church, you always went out to eat. When I asked what it all meant and why we did it, I was told that's just what we do. We go to church and then out to breakfast, because that's what the Kirchen's do! And this is what I would also do when I had my own family.

Now, I had one half-brother who was a born-again Christian and when he came over, he would always talk about Jesus, and how we need to accept Jesus as our Savior so that we could be saved. I remember one day he was talking about Jesus, and my dad let him know he did not need a Bible thumping Jesus freak in his house. If my brother wanted to stay, he could not talk about that Jesus stuff in his house anymore. So, when my brother talked to me about Jesus, I also did not want to listen or hear about it either, because neither did my dad.

My dad was also very racial, mean, prideful, and arrogant. He taught me to not like other races because they were worthless and stupid. He would always tell racial jokes and anyone who was not white and German got called something. He was a fighter all his life and would always intimidate others. He would even challenge other people if he felt they disrespected him or his family. He was my dad and I loved him, but I was also very afraid of him, because he would let me have it if I did something wrong. It didn't even matter where we were or who we were with. If I did something wrong, I got cracked. My dad was also a womanizer and taught me his outlook on women at a very young age. He told me what they were good for. He would have girlfriends on the side, and a few times I was with him when he would be with his girlfriends. Every time he was with another woman, he would say to me, "This is what men do, son. You have side chicks." He told me that anything I saw was between him and I, and to say nothing to anyone. He told me women or broads were only good for sex and if you married one, they should always be at home either cooking, cleaning, or in bed naked. After a while, he let me read his porno magazines, which I had already been sneaky about and looking at. He would have me check out other women with him, and he even had his side women show-off their bodies to me.

So, while growing up, these are the things I learned from my dad:

- There was no Jesus and people talking about Jesus were Bible thumping freaks.

- If you were not white, you were worthless.

- Germans were the only respectable race that can be trusted.

- Fight when you need to and make sure you win.

- Women were only good for certain things and nothing more.

- Always have a side chick.

- Always use your good looks and charm to get what you want.

- Never keep anyone too close.

- Always watch your back.

- And never answer to anyone.

So, for me to get to Jesus, not stay racial and eventually respect myself and others, my dad's death was inevitable. I believe if he had lived a normal life span, I would still be living as he taught me and probably not have accepted Jesus into my life. We were so close. I would have become who he was with all the same values and beliefs. As it turned out, I still inherited my dad's values and beliefs and lived that way for decades. Then, through wanting to change by seeking God and His direction, I was able to overcome those old ways and change my belief system.

Why did my mom choose her boyfriend over me and let me be homeless at age 14?

I was shown that I had to become homeless to be able to meet my future foster family. As I was homeless and bouncing around from couch to couch in L.A., I ended up in a home where other Christian men lived and they took me to church. This church was where I was introduced to my future foster family. I remember this family spoke with my half-brother who went to the same church, and offered to take me into their home for a one-week trial period. When my half-brother asked me if I wanted to go with them, it was a very surreal feeling for me, because it really solidified the fact that I was on my own and I wasn't ever going back home. I decided to go with them and eventually that week turned into two and soon after that, they asked if I wanted to stay with them.

During my time with that foster family, I experienced love and what a true family was. I was able to see God in their lives. I saw my foster family treat me and accept me as a part of their family. God used my foster family to teach me about Him and it was through my foster family that I started to read the Bible, learn about God, and accept Jesus into my life.

Everything that happened in my life started with my dad's death. He was the head, and as cruel as it may sound to some, I believe his death was part of my destiny. My dad was the one piece that would have hindered the course I was to take. If he had not died, I would not have become homeless, and probably not an addict, definitely not a stripper, or a porn star. His death started my testimony of God's amazing grace and mercy on my life, and without these whys, this book would not have been written.

As I look back on my childhood, I can truly say this—as hard, as tough, as lonely, as scary, and as crazy things were for me—I wouldn't change any of it.

This is my testimony—a testimony of who God is. It will be through my testimony, that others may get a chance to meet God and accept Jesus Christ into their lives.

If one person reading this book comes to know and accept Jesus into their heart and life, then I am truly grateful for everything that happened!

GOD'S GRACE

I now see, understand, and believe that my life had a predestined purpose given by God before I was conceived. The devil also knew I had a purpose and tried to take me out many times throughout my life, and I didn't even know it. But by the grace of God, I was covered and shielded from the devil and his ultimate plan to destroy me. Every situation the devil used to try and take me out, was thrown right back in his face and used to glorify the kingdom of God through this testimony of God's grace and love on my life.

Below are just a few incidents of God's grace upon my life, and how He covered me and shielded me for such a time as this. Any of these circumstances should have or could have killed me, made me incapacitated, or even made me dependent upon others. I ran hard, fast, and alone for most of my life, and I consumed alcohol, drugs, and steroids daily and weekly for many years. There is absolutely no medical reasoning behind my survival or present overall condition. The rules of life say I should either be dependent on medication, be dependent on machines, or not alive at all.

- Appendix burst, releasing poisons
- Saved from drowning in a pool

- Saved from choking to death

- Saved from being hit by a car

- Homeless and on the streets

- Involved in a high-speed chase with police

- Acute staph infection throughout my lower body

- Caught in 20-foot storm waves and saved from drowning

- Broken neck from a major car accident

- Acute alcohol poisoning

- Crazy gun battle with friends

- Alcohol and drug overdose

- Heavy alcohol consumption for over 30 days straight

- Skydiving—first shoot didn't open, and second shoot opened at 3000 feet

- While flying, the plane was hit by lightning, and fell 15,000 feet

- Assaulted and blacked out while on tour in Canada

- Diagnosed with Crohn's disease with over five feet of bad intestines

- Almost attacked by a rhino in South Africa

- Almost attacked by a baboon in South Africa

- Almost attacked by a lion in South Africa

- Assaulted in Cape Town, South Africa, for money and passport

- Cocaine overdose

- Cocaine, steroid, and alcohol poisoning

- Massive nosebleed while scuba diving with sharks and barracuda in Tahiti

- Bit by a brown recluse on left leg, needed surgery to remove flesh-eating poison

- Bit again by brown recluse on right hand, needed surgery to remove flesh- eating poison

- Bit again by brown recluse on left hand, poison traveled up arm, and up to heart. Was rushed to doctor and given antibiotic, along with surgery, to remove flesh-eating poisons

- Meth overdose from a five day run

- Cocaine and alcohol blackout

- Jumped out of a car at 40 mph in a rage

- Diagnosed with an enlarged heart and an irregular heartbeat

- Diagnosed as having a stroke

- Heavy crack cocaine consumption for 60 days straight

This is in no way the complete list of times the divine presence of God kept me, and some may argue and say I got lucky, but I have spoken to numerous medically trained specialists and the word *lucky* was never spoken. But what was said over and over was this, "You shouldn't be alive. You shouldn't be able to do what you do. You shouldn't look like you do." And every person concluded with, "You definitely have someone watching over you."

Well, that someone is God!

UNEXPECTED GIFT

A t this stage of my life, I had just left Washington State, where I reunited with my foster family after almost 30 years. Being back with my foster family was very cool to me and I really enjoyed it, until it opened up old hurts and unresolved issues. I didn't know how to deal with this. All my old coping skills resurfaced and once again, I felt like I was going crazy. I was about to knock on death's door one more time. During this time, I felt this overwhelming need that I had to get back to California and I didn't know why. I had nothing in California to return to. The only thing that was there was my old life, or so I thought.

I left Washington State very abruptly. I left my job, my belongings, and I left everything with only enough money for a plane ticket and three nights in a motel. I decided to fly into Long Beach and stay somewhere along the Pacific Coast Highway, so I could visit my biological mom, who was now living in a convalescent home. When I arrived in Long Beach, it was about 9 p.m. The plan was to visit my mom in the morning, then look up some old friends and try to hustle up a place to stay, because I only had three days to find a place before my money ran out.

After a few days in Long Beach and visiting my mom, I made my way to Huntington Beach. I briefly stayed in Huntington Beach and then decided to head to Van Nuys, where I could stay for a while. When I finally got to Van Nuys, I got settled in and was trying to find a job. While I was on the computer, I decided to look at dating sites. Now, this was something I had never done before, but for some reason, I felt pulled to do it.

After looking at many pictures, one woman stood out the most. I remember looking at her picture and thinking she was very attractive, but there was something different about her and didn't know what this was. I read her profile, which was different for me, because I didn't care about the profiles, only the pictures. As I was reading her profile, I saw she was a Christian, and when I saw that I remember thinking to myself, *I wonder if she would take me to church?* That was really all I wanted from anyone at that point, just to get back to church. I was so tired of my life and all the mess and I just wanted to get back to God and I needed someone to help me get there. When we finally spoke on the phone, I think my first question to her was just that, "Can I go to church with you?"

We spoke every day after that and I went to church with her that following Sunday. Over the next few months, we became very close. We were either going to church, going to eat, going shopping, or just hanging out and talking. I wanted what she had. I wanted to know God like she did. She was a prayer warrior and knew the word and I wanted that. No matter where we were at, we would somehow end up talking about God, the Bible, and prayer. She took me to conferences and Bible studies, and she would pray with me over the phone every morning and every night. She brought me a Bible, she brought me confession books, and she was all in with the process of helping me in my return to God.

Over the course of the next year, there were many times I struggled to make it financially, and during those times I never wanted to tell her what I was going through. The amazing thing was that she seemed to always know those times and would just show up to my place with just the right thing at just the right time. She always made sure I was okay and had what I needed. I really didn't understand why she was doing these things for me, considering we were not dating or having sex. I remember many times asking her why she did the things she did and her answer was always the same—God told me to.

She was always there for me. It didn't matter if I was being mean, or if I had just slipped up and got loaded, she was there. She either talked me through it or picked me up out of my mess, and she always did it in love. She loved me when I didn't deserve any love, and she loved me when no one else would. She would love me even after I would disappear for days and not talk to her. It didn't matter what I did—she was there. I remember asking her again, "Why? Why are you still here?" and her answer was always the same—God told me to. Eventually I asked her to be my girlfriend, and even with everything going on, she said yes.

I would like to tell you that after that, things got better, but they did not. We still had some issues because of my old behavior, but we would seek God through it all. She stuck with me even when her friends told her to leave, and she even lost some friends because she stuck with me. She was there through it all and every time I fell, she would tell me to get back up. "Let's go," she'd say, "Don't let the devil win. Don't let the devil take you out." She would always tell me that I had a purpose and that God wanted to use me to help others. She would always say there were people I was supposed to help through my testimony and the devil knew this, too. And to stop listening to him. She would then tell me who I was in Christ and confess those words over me. She was my rock and I thank God for putting this woman in my life. I am also so thankful she had the ear to hear and was obedient to what God was saying to her about me. She never gave up, and she was strong when I was weak. She prayed for me when I didn't know I needed prayer, and she was my helpmate before I knew what that meant. She was a strong, godly woman, full of love, no matter how unlovable I was. She was a prayer warrior that could pray heaven down, very discerning, and an incredible fighter. She was who God put in my life and I didn't even know it.

One Friday afternoon, while on my lunch break from work, we had gone out to eat, and on our way back to my job, my body went completely limp. I couldn't talk or raise my hands. I dropped my wallet on the floor and was hunched over, not being able to move. When she saw what was happening to me, she rushed me to the ER, and when the emergency staff saw me, they immediately started running tests and soon after that, admitted me into the hospital as a stroke patient. I had no idea what was going on and wasn't taking anything real seriously, because up to this point, I had always bounced back from any serious life issues. But this time was different. I wasn't the same. I wasn't myself. I felt very weak and had no control of my body.

While all this was going on, she called on the church to start a prayer chain and all the warriors began to pray for me. She had her friends praying for me and these were people I had only known for a short time, but they were coming to the hospital and laying hands on me in prayer. On that Sunday, the church held a special intercessory prayer for my healing and all the while, she stayed with me by my side in prayer and belief for my healing. She even brought me food, so I wouldn't have to eat what the hospital had to offer. Sunday night, I went to sleep still having problems with my speech and could barely hold my arms or legs up. When Monday morning came, I woke up and was perfectly fine. I had no signs of a stroke. The doctors ran the same tests they had run Friday and this time, the test results showed nothing wrong. The doctors had me do a stress test and it came back normal. Everything was normal. There were no signs of a stroke and not one doctor could explain my miraculous recovery.

I can certainly explain this. That healing was from the power of prayer.

Shortly after this occurred, I decided to get some real help and turn my life around for God. I decided to go away and move into a place that was God- centered to find what I was looking for. While I was away, she would come by to see me every weekend to support me and go to church with me. I vividly remember one specific day when she had come by to visit. We were walking and talking and I said I felt like I was supposed to become a pastor and share the gospel, but I was just not sure. When that statement came out of my mouth, a sparrow landed on my chest, right over my heart and just stayed there. It must have stayed on my chest for a good 30 seconds or so. We both just stopped and stared at it while it flapped its wings to stay on my chest. Now, here I am trying to determine if what I am feeling is correct, and an actual sparrow lands on my chest. I will have to say that wasn't just a coincidence. That was a sign from God that my feelings were correct.

And as for *she*, well, soon after that, she became my wife and I count myself very blessed to be able to call her my wife. God knew all along what I needed and who I was to be with. I left Washington State and headed to California on a feeling, not knowing that God had my wife and helpmate waiting for me, on a dating site, in Van Nuys, California.

BAPTIZED WITH
ANGELS

For *He will command His angels in regard to you, to protect and defend and guard you in all your ways. – Psalm 91:11 (AMP)*

One summer day in July, my wife and I were baptized together. A few Sundays before the baptism, our church gave an altar call for anyone who needed prayer. So, my wife and I went up to receive prayer. The reason we went up was because our marriage was being threatened and we weren't doing well as a couple. The person praying with us asked what we needed prayer for and we told him. After the prayer, we were asked about baptism. Now, my wife and I had both been baptized before, but the urge to do it again was very strong for me and at that time, it was suggested that both my wife and I get baptized together. We prayed for the answer and both of us heard *yes,* so we scheduled the baptism. Later that week, we were informed that they were not going to be baptizing on the scheduled day, so we rescheduled for the next opening which happened to be a Saturday night. Wow—what a night that night would turn out to be, and for a minute, it almost didn't happen.

A few days before the baptism, I remember being upset that it had been rescheduled and was starting to have a change of heart about going through with it. In the days leading up to it, my wife and I were really going through tough times with each other. All of my issues and feelings from my past were coming up and the devil was really trying to keep division between my wife and I. He was trying to discourage me from the whole baptism thing. I was really trying to work through some things about myself, my past careers, my failures, my addictions, and the relationship with my wife, but the harder I tried to fix, change, or forget things, the worse everything seemed to get. My mind was scrambled with all these thoughts, thoughts of why do this again, why get baptized, why try to mend this relationship, why keep going to church, and the one thought that kept coming up was that even if I got baptized again, nothing was going to change. Later, I realized all that chatter of defeat was the enemy trying to keep me from that life-changing, belief-strengthening, and signs and wonders day of baptism.

I still remember the night before the baptism. I was restless and I had this stirring in my gut. Then I felt anxious, nervous, excited, and apprehensive all at once. In my head, I was playing back the other time I was baptized and how nothing happened, or so I thought. It had been decades since I was first baptized, and I thought once you were baptized everything changed. I thought everything turned for the better, and with no problems, since all I ever saw or heard of people after they had been baptized was this ah-ha moment. They always made it seem like everything was different for them and that their lives were a bed of roses from that moment on.

Well, that was not the case for me after my first baptism. A lot of things happened in my life after the fact—things like abandonment, stripping, porn, sex, drugs, alcohol, divorce, loss of jobs, renting rooms, living in motels, hopelessness, depression, thoughts of suicide, thoughts of homicide, and so on. So, this time, for this baptism, I was ready for change and I came expecting. I was expecting God to show Himself and to feel His presence. I knew inside that if nothing happened it would just be another experience of disappointment for me and at this point, I would have probably just given up on the whole God thing. So, all day, leading up to the baptism, I was praying and talking to God. Over and over I would say, "I'm expecting to see something, God. Show me who you are. For real, show me something." For me, at this time in my life, I needed a sign. Yes, I had been healed before, and yes, I should have OD'd many times before. Yes, I could have been killed many times before, and again yes, I always seemed to make it through tough times, but at this moment my faith was low and my belief was weak. When it came to faith and belief, I heard many people say that *you have to know that you know*, and I didn't have that know that you know in me at that time. So, I admitted my weakness of faith and belief to God and I pleaded with Him, asking Him that on this day He'd please show me Himself. I really needed something, and I desperately wanted to feel a change in my life. I wanted to come out of that water knowing He was my Father and I was His child and that He was for real and that He did love me. That was my expectation and I was not going to accept anything less.

I had met a man from the church that I had become friends with and we would talk on a regular basis. I gave him a call to let him know that my wife and I were being baptized that Saturday and that I would like him to be there. He told me he wouldn't be able to attend, but that he would let other members know who we were and to look out for us. When we arrived at the church, the leaders had everyone getting baptized meet in the hallway. Then they gave us the rundown of what was to happen, handed us our gowns, and told us to get changed. As I was changing in the dressing room, I started to get nervous and then found myself saying over and over again, "Come on, God, show me something."

As we lined up for baptism, I counted about ten others also getting baptized, some for the first time and others to rededicate themselves. My wife and I watched each person as they got baptized and as each person came out of the water, I wondered how these people were feeling, if anything happened to them, if they were changed for good, and if they now knew God was with them. I even pondered the idea that now these people would have no more sin. Now I know that as a Christian, we will always sin. In fact, some of us will sin multiple times before even getting dressed in the morning, but I wanted freedom. Freedom to know that I know for real, for real, that God was with me.

Next up to the baptism pool was my wife and I, and as we got into the water we were asked if we were ready to come before God as a couple and we were. My wife was first up, and as they held her, this was said, "I baptize you in the name of the Father, the Son, and the Holy Spirit." Into the water she went, and when she came out, she looked the same. I thought I would see something happen when she came out of the water, but I saw nothing. She just looked wet. Then it was my turn. As I got ready to go under the water, I had this rush of anticipation and expectation that something miraculous was going to happen. The two men held me and again, this was said, "I baptize you in the name of the Father, the Son, and the Holy Spirit." And under I went. While under the water, I felt this feeling I can't explain. There were sounds under the water, also, that I can't explain.

When I came up out of the water, I did a quick self–examination and nothing. Nothing happened. I remember getting out of the water and telling myself, *Okay, here we go again, one more time. I'm clean and I have a new start on life.* I didn't feel any miraculous change and was very disappointed, because I was expecting God to show up in a big way. I started thinking to myself, *Man, what were you thinking? You were expecting some big thing to happen, and all you did was get your hopes up for something and one more time nothing happened, so now what.* I realize now that those thoughts were planted be the enemy. He gave me the thought and I bit the bait and ran with it. At that moment, I didn't take every thought captive as the word says we should in 2 Corinthians 10:5.

When it was all over, my wife and I got in the car, and we decided to stop and eat before we drove back home. We stopped at this little walk-up Mexican restaurant. When we parked, she decided she didn't want to eat. In fact, she stayed in the car because she was still upset with me. She even stated that we should still probably separate. I did not want to hear any of that, especially after we had just got baptized, so I got out of the car and ordered my food. I waited a bit before getting back in the car and when I did an amazing thing happened. This overwhelming smell of incense followed me into the car and pretty soon the whole car was overtaken by it. My wife noticed it first and said, "That's incense!

Oh my, that's God and He's all over you!" The smell and fog became so strong we eventually had to pull over, roll down the windows, and sit for a while until it was gone.

About a week after the baptism, my friend texted me two photos that his friends had taken of my wife and I getting baptized. I looked at them thinking it was pretty cool that my wife and I had done this together, so I showed them to my wife and that was it. A few days after that, I remember sitting on the bed reading the word and hoping that things had changed, that this time being baptized was different, and that I was finally free. As I sat there, I heard God say, "Look at the picture of your baptism again," so, I pulled the picture up again and looked at it. Nothing special. It was the same picture and then I heard, "Look in the water." I looked at the picture again and there they were—angels in the water!

I was in awe. I just stared at the picture. I didn't know what to think. I remember saying, "Is that really what I think it is?" I had angels in the water with me, one very clearly below my back in the water. As soon as my wife got home, I showed her the picture again. I asked her to look in the water, and then she saw the angels. She immediately got teary-eyed and said, "Wow, look at God."

This picture just reconfirmed that God is real, that angels are with us, and that heaven is awaiting us. I truly hope my story and this picture will help everyone and anyone having doubt or unbelief come to the saving knowledge of Jesus Christ.

WHO AM I?

I remember the day my mentor asked me the question, "Who is Kevin?" I was shocked when he asked that because he made me really think. I had always lived my life day to day, moving and shuffling as I saw fit, always trying to fly below the radar, or just fit in. So, when he asked that question my answer was easy, because it was a well-rehearsed answer that went something like this, "Well, I was a foster kid, my dad died when I was 12, and my mom kicked me out at 14. I was homeless for a while, and then a church family let me stay with them. A few years after that, I became a Chippendales dancer, and after that I was a porn star. After Chippendales and porn, I worked in sales and I have been in sales and management ever since. I have no real family except my wife, I do have a son, but I haven't seen him very much at all. We don't have much of a relationship, but that's not because I haven't tried. So there it is—that's it—that's me."

Obviously, my response did not answer the question of *Who is Kevin?* because he responded with, "That's all good, but who is the real Kevin? Who is the Kevin God says he is?" When it finally sunk in that my answer didn't answer anything and that I really didn't know who I was, it was very frustrating for me. Here I am being asked who I am and I didn't know. I had always associated who I was with what I had done, experienced, or accomplished, whether it be good or bad. I never had a true identity of myself. From a very young age, I was trained to be something else or someone else than me. I was taught to not show emotions, to be seen and not heard, to just get along, to just blend in, and adapt to any situation or occasion.

Not only did I not know who Kevin was, but after more questions I realized I didn't even know what made me happy, what made me sad, and I didn't even know what I liked or disliked. I had never been asked who I was or what made me happy and sad before. Throughout my life, people told me what *they* thought of me or who *they* thought I was as a person and they really had no idea of who I was, because they were forming an opinion based on a made-up person. Whether good or bad, I had made myself and changed myself so much that no one including myself really knew the real Kevin.

During this barrage of unpleasant questioning, I realized that my answers to what I liked, disliked, and what made me happy and sad were also made up. Throughout my years, I had made a mental filling cabinet of answers to pull from when I was asked these types of questions. I would study and listen to people knowing that certain questions might come up, so by the time I was asked a question, I had already figured out what the other person was all about and just adapted my answer to fit what I thought they would want to hear. It wasn't that I was intentionally lying or manipulating them. I was just in survival mode to blend in, fit in, or deflect further questions. Throughout my teens and way into my adulthood, I was always living as that unaccepted kid who just wanted to be accepted.

Adapting and fitting myself into someone else's life was what I knew how to do, and I was very good at it. I had been doing that my whole life and had mastered it so well that the answers I gave seemed to be, not only genuine to the other person, but also to me. So being asked these questions at this time in my life was hard, but knowing I couldn't blend into what he wanted to hear was even harder. I was now in unchartered waters because not only was this man my mentor, but he was a very close friend, and not being able to answer these questions as I normally had done throughout my life was really uncomfortable. I knew that he knew I didn't know the answers.

When I left his office, I was hit with the reality and sadness that I had lived my whole life completely disconnected from everything and everyone, including myself. I lived my whole life in a self-protecting, self-medicating, self-sabotaging, and people-pleasing place that had no real meaning. I lived the desperado lifestyle, never attaching to anything or anyone—a professional chameleon.

While I was writing this chapter about who I was, God revealed to me that I had basically lived my entire life as the *Unknown Flasher*, the act I performed at Chippendales. While wearing a costume with a bag on my head, he showed me that being completely hidden as the flasher was a comfortable spot for me and I had been living as that character my entire life. For me, this was simply—I could see you, but you couldn't see me. People thought they were looking at me and talking to me, but it wasn't me. It was the chameleon who blended into life's situations. I could become anyone at the flip of a switch and I learned how to do that at a very young age for acceptance and protection. We are talking decades of self-deceit and self-lies, all to feel some kind of normalcy. How crazy is that?

But it was true. My crazy was what I thought was normal. All I wanted was acceptance and approval and my prior life experiences had proven to me that if you really knew who I was, you would ultimately leave me. So, I never let anyone get too close or too personal with me, and by doing that, I either pushed people away because everything was getting too emotionally uncomfortable, or they left because I made myself this detached emotionally unreachable person. When life became too real or people got too close, I always chose to get high, drunk, or both and disappear—thus, sabotaging the relationship. Either way, every relationship or friendship I attempted to have I destroyed because I didn't want anyone to get close enough to know or see the real me. I tried to hide every emotion—sadness, loneliness, happiness, anger, fear, and so on. I had pushed my emotions so far down that I was usually perceived as the guy that really didn't care about anyone or anything. I was so far from my own reality that I didn't even know or see the real me when I looked in the mirror. I was this empty shell that had skin, muscle, bone, and a heartbeat. I only thought I was looking at the real me, but really what I was looking at was this made-up person, and not the real Kevin. So, who was the real Kevin?

Who did God say the real Kevin was? Now, that was the question.

While meeting with my mentor, he gave me a homework assignment. He wanted me to find out who the real Kevin was, not who I thought I was or what my past said I was, and certainly not who society said I was, but who God said I was. He had me go to the Bible and find scripture on who God said I was. He knew that I had not completely let go of my past or the old Kevin, and he even told me the devil wanted to keep me trapped in the past, but the longer I stayed in the past the longer I would miss my future.

All the doubt and unbelief in myself was created by the devil, speaking in my ear, and then I'd listen and then accept the lies. These lies kept me right where he wanted me—trapped in the bondage and in the belief that I was nothing but an ex-stripping, porn star who had done a lot of drugs and wasted his life. The devil had me believing that no one would ever truly love me, respect me, believe in me, or stand by me. The devil is the master of lies and deception. He got me to believe that I was un-lovable, unwanted, and a social outcast. Since my biological father left me, what would stop God from leaving me? He got me to believe that since my mom chose someone else to love, rather than me, that every-one else including God would do the same thing. He had me believing that God was no different than my parents. Wow, what a bunch of lies! I knew I needed to let go of the past if I was to ever be free and move forward.

Through reading the scripture, I found out that I had a new identity in Christ and that God predestined me for something great. God had truly forgiven me for all the things I had done and what the devil meant for harm, God was using for His glory. I had been saved by grace and not by deeds. He chose me before birth for a purpose and every promise in the Bible was mine. As I sat down and looked through the Bible to find out who God said I was, I found scripture after scripture clearly stating who I was and my true identity in Christ. I have listed a few of them below:

- According to scripture, I am a New Creation – 2 Corinthians 5:17 (NASB)

- According to scripture, I am Loved – Jeremiah 31:3 (NASB)

- According to scripture, I am Special – Ephesians 2:10 (NASB)

- According to scripture, I am Precious – 1 Corinthians 6:20 (NASB)

- According to scripture, I am Unique – Psalm 139:13 (NASB)

- According to scripture, I am Important – 1 Peter 2:9 (NASB)

- According to scripture, I have a Purpose – Jeremiah 29:11 (NASB)

- According to scripture, I am His – Isaiah 43:1 (NASB)

So now, whenever the devil tries to come at me through my past, I don't listen because I don't know who he is talking about. The person he's still talking about is a dead man!

Scripture says: Therefore, if anyone is in Christ, he is a new creature; the old things have passed away; behold, new things have come. – 2 Corinthians 5:17 (NASB)

The devil is a liar and can't even speak truth, and according to scripture, the truth is not in him. – John 8:44 (NASB)

So, who is the real Kevin?

Kevin is redeemed, loved, special, precious, unique, and important. My life has a purpose and I know what my purpose is. I know God loves me and I am His, and I am an heir to the kingdom, adopted in and through Christ. I know I can do *all things* through Christ who strengthens me.

Best of all, I know I am saved and that heaven awaits me.

If you are reading this and don't know who you are in Christ, like I didn't, I want to encourage you to memorize a few of the scriptures I listed above or some others that tell you who you are. Start confessing them over yourself, get them in your heart, and renew your mind with them. Not if, but *when* the devil tries to come at you with his lies or tries to bring up your past, you can beat him down with God's word of who you really are.

IGNORING GOD VS.
HONORING GOD

That, in reference to your former manner of life, you lay aside the old self, which is being corrupted in accordance with the lusts of deceit, and that you be renewed in the spirit of your mind,[24] and put on the new self, which in *the likeness of* God has been created in righteousness and holiness of the truth. – Ephesians 4:22-24 (NASB)

While writing this book, I was repeatedly attacked by the devil to get off track so I would not finish it or publish it. I can honestly say some attacks I saw as just that and got through them, and others I didn't see. I allowed them to get to me. Then there were attacks that I didn't even recognize as an attack and allowed my old thoughts and ideas of who I used to be, win out. Even with all the studying, counseling, and mentoring, I fell prey to the deceit and lies of the devil and I allowed those old thoughts and my pride to again produce havoc in my life.

One Sunday, while attending church, I received a huge revelation regarding my life and how I was living. The speaker was talking about the book of Romans 1:18-32, Romans 2:1-16 (MSG) and it really convicted me. I had not been living as I should. Oh, sure I was praying, and reading and studying the word. I was even talking to random people about God, but I wasn't truly sold out for God. I wasn't allowing Him to control everything and I wasn't willing to completely die to self and let go of the old man. I hadn't completely given God my all through prayer, worship, praise, devotion, or obedience. I didn't have an intimate relationship with Him, but what I had was religion. See, I still to some extent, enjoyed the old man and certain sinful things, and I still trusted myself and my ideas more than completely relying on Him, His plans, and His ways. I still idolized my thoughts, and escaped reality by living in my mind. I was either reliving the past or fantasizing in the future, and at times, I was just in complete lala land.

Vain imaginations is what the Bible calls it. I not only idolized my thoughts, but I also idolized myself. I was still running my life and not fully submitting to God and His ways. I was relying consciously or unconsciously on my old ways, habits, or addictions when having to cope or face something. That was my comfortable spot or so I thought, when in reality it was death, because you can't serve two masters.

One morning, I was reading and meditating on those scriptures in the book of Romans when God spoke to me very sternly saying, "Look back on your life and how you have lived." He directed me towards Romans 1:21 (KJV) and the scripture jumped out at me as if the words were ten times bigger than any of the others.

Because that, when they knew God, they glorified him not as God, neither were thankful; but became vain in their imaginations, and their foolish heart was darkened.

Wow! God was showing me that the way I was living was not glorifying Him. While I sat quietly in the presence of God, He showed me things about myself. He showed me that all the things I prayed to be removed from my life were removed, and all the prayers for addictions to be broken had been broken. He showed me that I was still operating in many ways, as the old man. He also reminded me about free will. So even though He broke the chains of bondage from my life, I still had the choice to return to these chains because of my free will. It wasn't that

He had not answered my prayers. Rather, it was that I made a choice to continue in my old ways rather than completely die to self and move towards the uncomfortable unknown and choose freedom. This uncomfortable and unknown freedom was a scary place for me since that meant giving up old habits, but holding on to the old me and my old ideas eventually ended in some kind of self-inflicted bondage.

God said, "Look back. What have your wants, your ways, your thoughts, your beliefs, your ego, your pride, your habits, or addictions produced? Was there ever any long, sustainable happiness in anything you did?" I can't explain the feeling that produced inside of me and it was a harsh reality to know that I relied and trusted myself more than Him. It was time to surrender and stop escaping into my mind. It was time to stop thinking I was something I wasn't, or that I was owed something, deserved something, or should be respected in any way considering how I had lived my life. It was time for me to completely let go of the old man, the old ways, the old pleasures, and seek God. And seeking God meant I had to die, and choose Him and His ways over mine. My life was to be no more. It was time to glorify Him for what He had done for me, to focus on Him, and do what He asked of me.

While I was meditating on this, God spoke again and brought me back to the scripture in Ephesians 4:22-24 and this time I read it from the (MSG) version.

Since, then, we do not have the excuse of ignorance, everything—and I do mean everything—connected with that old way of life has to go. It's rotten through and through. Get rid of it! And then take on an entirely new way of life—a God-fashioned life, a life renewed from the inside and working itself into your conduct as God accurately reproduces his character in you.

He also spoke to me letting me know to not just seek Him when things are bad or challenging, but to also seek Him when things are good.

Scripture says: In all your ways acknowledge Him, And He will make your paths straight. – Proverbs 3:6 (NASB)

Yes, it was time to completely put off the old man and put on the new man, and this made me very uncomfortable. I had lived with the old man for my whole life and now, to have complete reliance on God in all my ways, rather than on me was uncomfortable and unimaginable.

So, I needed to completely surrender to God and die to self. I was okay surrendering to God, but dying to self, well, that proved to be easier said than done. Even with the proof of my life before my eyes, I continued to trust myself and my thoughts more than God. How crazy was that?

As I was meditating on this, God brought me to Proverbs 3:5 (NASB).

Trust in the *Lord* with all your heart And do not lean on your own understanding.

It was time to have an intimate relationship with God, but what is that and what does that look like? He showed me that an intimate relationship takes time to build and grow. When someone desires to be with another person, that person will constantly seek out the other person— texting, calling, finding time and ways to pursue the other person. People will even stop certain behaviors to respect or keep the other person in their life. But what about God? I needed to pursue and seek Him in the same way and give up certain behaviors. This meant I needed to be in a relentless pursuit for an intimate relationship with Him. No more half measures. He showed me that when someone really desires a true intimate relationship with another person, they are constantly finding time to be alone with that person, to learn more about that person, to connect closer with that person, to know their voice in a crowded room, and that's what God wanted from me.

As my quiet time was ending, He said one more thing that changed me and my stubbornness towards complete submission. He said, "You have never seen the full potential of your life because you haven't fully died to yourself yet." Then He said, "Fully submit to me in all your ways and see what I will do."

When I heard this, I immediately said, "Okay, I will do that." But then I thought, *Wait, do what?* So, I asked God what that looked like and once again, He brought me to scripture—James 4:7-8 (NASB).

Submit therefore to God. Resist the devil and he will flee from you. Draw near to God and He will draw near to you. Cleanse your hands, you sinners; and purify your hearts, you double-minded.

Then He went on to say, "Keep renewing your mind with my word and think only on these things."

> *Whatever is true, whatever is honorable, whatever is right, whatever is pure, whatever is lovely, whatever is of good repute, if there is any excellence and if anything worthy of praise, dwell on these things. The things you have learned and received and heard and seen in me, practice these things, and the God of peace will be with you. – Philippians 4:8-9 (NASB)*

I can say this—I truly understand the importance of keeping sober-minded and alert for any tricks and schemes of the devil that can get me off track. Now when I see them, I see them for what they are—stupid tricks!

I am understanding more and more that we don't fight in the flesh, but in the spirit. We can't beat the devil in our own strength. We have to pray, use the word, and use our God-given spiritual authority. We have been given all the power and dominion over everything and the word of God has the power to dismantle and expose the lies and tricks of the evil one. As we do this, we remind ourselves of *who* we are and *whose* we are and then let's have some fun and remind the devil of his future! We are God's chosen, we are royalty, and are headed to heaven to be with Jesus. As for you, devil, well, you are headed to hell where you will burn forever. Sorry!

CONCLUSION
MY PURPOSE...

As I finish writing this book, I have to say my life has completely changed. I no longer see myself as that unwanted loser who accomplished nothing except being an unloving, unlovable, drug addict—amounting to nothing but a retired stripper and ex porn star who no one wanted around. I now see myself as loved, and the amazing thing is, that even though as a kid I was never adopted, I can now say I have been adopted! Adopted by God as one of His children—how about that!

I now see myself as fearfully and wonderfully made in the image of God and that whatever I went through, good or bad, all had a purpose. I had no idea that the game I was playing and the pain I carried as a child into adulthood, along with the destructive life I lived for decades, was actually going to be used for a purpose. This purpose was to show God's glory through my story. An old life that had gone nowhere, was heading nowhere, and had produced nothing, was now being used to advance the kingdom of God. My game and pain turned out to be my purpose.

Today, I have the opportunity to lead others to Christ, and minister to the hurt and broken. I have been blessed to be the founder of a non-profit organization, ROC, that helps provide housing and a variety of daily needs for foster kids that have aged-out of the system, with no place to go.

Today, I have been blessed with a beautiful wife and a family who loves me unconditionally.

Today, I am being trained up for pastoral ministry, deliverance ministry, and to be used by God to help others go through and get through their circumstances with victory. Helping others find peace and meaning for their lives, helping them understand that God is love, and that no one is unworthy, unlovable, or unsavable is an amazing gift from God that I am truly thankful for.

Today, I have complete faith and belief in God. I know He only wants the best for me and I know He will never leave me or forsake me no matter what, and knowing this is my greatest peace.

Today, I have a circle of friends I can speak to about anything. I can share my thoughts or actions and know that they will listen without judgement. They will be there to support me, counsel me, and pray with me. They will always tell me the truth, no matter what, and even get in my mess if need be.

My prayer is that everyone and anyone reading this book—man, woman, young adult, or child—will find that one God-fearing person who will be *the one* to walk alongside them, through all the roses and thorns of life. Someone who will act and speak in truth and love, someone who will not judge, but love no matter what.

In closing, I would like to say this—any life that has been ripped apart by loss, abuse, abandonment, betrayal, alcohol, drugs, sex, anger, violence, or the like can be renewed and redeemed by the loving hand of God and the blood of Jesus Christ.

If you have read this book and do not know Jesus, but feel the gentle tug on your heart to accept Him into your life right now, say this prayer with me:

Jesus, I confess that I am a sinner and I am asking for forgiveness. I want you in my life, I believe you died for my sins, I believe that you were raised from the dead and that you are Lord. Today, I want you and accept you into my life to guide me and protect me. In Jesus' name I pray, amen.

If you said this prayer for the first time, you are now saved and now royalty!

Welcome to the family!

If you read this book and you have fallen away and want to recommit your life to Jesus, just tell Him, and remember He never left you, you left Him. Tell Him you want to come home. He will welcome you with open arms!

Thank you for your time in reading my story and testimony of who God is and how God, not only changed my life, but protected and covered me for a time as this. If He can do it for me, He can surely do the same for you!

God bless you all,

Kevin Kirchen